OK NOW WHAT?
A CAREGIVER'S GUIDE TO WHAT MATTERS

BY

SUE COLLINS R.N. & NANCY TAYLOR ROBSON

To All the best!
Sue Collins

1

Dedicated to friends, family, loved ones and caregivers past, present and future.

Introduction

What matters most when someone close to you has been diagnosed as terminal? Time and quality of life for both of you while coping with both the practical and emotional questions of this challenging passage.

We are all just walking each other home, according to Ram Dass. Whether you believe that there is life beyond this one or not, the reality is: our lives here are finite. We are all going to die one day, yet every death is individual – as is the walk toward that individual death both for the one leaving and for the ones they leave behind.

Focusing on what truly matters between human beings while taking care of the business of living at the end of life is what this book is about. It offers practical, experienced-based advice and tips on handling physical changes. It gives you resources for finding help when you need it. But it also tells some of the stories of others who have made this journey as caregivers, as family, friends, partners, spouses and neighbors, stories that will help to calm and encourage you and to let you know you are not alone.

A terminal diagnosis can be isolating. It produces an automatic category-shift in attitude by the people around the diagnosee from *person* to *patient*, from *us*, who are healthy and staying here for a while longer to *those* who are not, which is why so many choose to keep it a secret. Some people will look at the patient with smug sympathy, or even fear, as though a terminal diagnosis were contagious. Others will avoid the person, afraid to embarrass themselves or worse, hurt the person by saying or doing the wrong thing. Neither is useful or welcome. The person who has suddenly become a patient still wants and *needs* to be treated first and foremost as a person, a soul who needs normal human contact and as close to a normal life as he or she can manage despite changes in abilities, energy, appetite, interests and more.

Regardless of his or her relationship to the patient, the caregiver can feel isolated too. The person who will be the primary caregiver has, in all likelihood, not been trained for this new and at times overwhelming job. He or she often gets forgotten in this equation, yet needs just as much support, encouragement, and practical help as the person who has been diagnosed.

This book offers:

- Practical tips for coping with the physical changes that will impact both the person and the caregiver emotionally, physically, financially and spiritually.
- Advice on what to put in place before the person dies to make things a little easier for those they leave behind.
- The stories and examples of others to let people know they are not alone.
- Advice and tips for those who are not going to be primary caregiver, but who are friends, neighbors, colleagues or any other part of the relationships we all share in life.

There is no perfect way to walk through this time. (There's no perfect way to walk through all of life for that matter). But there are good ways to do it. Focusing on what really matters while taking care of the practical business of living and dying can make this journey slightly less scary and more rewarding for everyone.

How to use this book

Browse the chapter headings; skip around in the TIPS for ways to approach or solve specific problems. Search the *Sources* lists at the end of the chapters for additional information on a question or need. Read the stories of others' experiences. For the co-worker, friend or neighbor, this book offers advice and helpful hints on what to say or do as well as what not to say or do. For the loved one, spouse, and relative it's a practical guide to what you might expect at each stage and offers realistic and reasonable coping strategies. It includes examples born of the experience of a range of people – professionals in the field as well as non-professionals like yourself – of what you might experience on this difficult journey.

Yet, as we've said, each death is individual just as are the relationships, personalities and personal dynamics involved. Despite the individuality of experience, there are also issues and threads that are universal in human life. This book can act as a practical guide, an encouraging friend, and pragmatic support so that you and your loved one can have the best experience possible in the circumstances as you walk someone home.

Across America, 43.5 million people, (nearly one in five adults) care for a loved one 50 or older according to AARP.

The Writers:

Sue Collins has been a nurse for 39 years and a hospice nurse for 29 years. She has the extensive experience of the professional caregiver and has seen virtually everything at the end of life. This book arises out of the OMG!-I-can't-believe-they-said-that/did-that moments she's dealt with as well as the anger, frustration, grace and poignancy she has witnessed during the last days of patients for whom she has cared.

Nancy Taylor Robson, author of three other books, lost her father to bone cancer, which took approximately three years from diagnosis to departure, and her mother-in-law to a long decline and a series of strokes. She has sat by the deathbeds of treasured friends and seen more than one through the last months, weeks, days and hours of life. She knows that as painful a journey as this is, there can be gifts and blessings along the way. AND, she knows, (at least intellectually), that none of us is getting out of here alive.

TABLE OF CONTENTS

Chapter One

THE OH SHIT MOMENT

The reality is: Life here is finite. For every single one of us. Yet most of us manage to forget that fact or bury it somewhere deep in our psyches and carry on as though we had all the time in the world. We don't. We are all leaving here at some point. A terminal diagnosis means that the person diagnosed as terminal is most likely leaving sooner rather than later. What that means for the person and for those who care for them is complex.

Whether it's the progression of a disease that has been in a holding pattern, the inevitable result of an aging body or a sudden awakening to a symptom that turns out to be way more than anyone anticipated, a terminal diagnosis is a shock. It's the Oh Shit Moment, the one that none of us is ever *really* prepared for. Spouse, friend, partner, colleague, parent or (God forbid) child, our reactions to the news that it's terminal are often the same.

This can't be happening! It's not real; it can't be. This can't be right; it's too soon! There must be some mistake! The first reaction when someone we care about is given a terminal diagnosis is disbelief. Then fear. Anger. Then the questions begin. It's terminal, what does that mean? How long until…? What will it look like? What will it feel like? Will there be pain? Do we really want to know? How the heck did we get here? Is someone to blame for this? Could it have been prevented? This is unfair! This can't be happening! Oh *shit*! Now what?!

Our long habit of living ill-prepares us for dying. The disbelief and fear of a terminal diagnosis are hard enough when it's someone in their 60's, 70's or older. It's something else when the person is, like Carla's son, Brad, in the prime of his life.

> *When Brad phoned his mother with the news that he had just received a diagnosis of Stage 4 cancer, Carla, who lived in another city, immediately got in her car. She was determined to join him for whatever would happen next. On the way, she phoned a longtime friend whose office she would pass.*
>
> *'I'm on the road. Brad just phoned. It's Stage 4 cancer," she said without preamble.*
>
> *Emily tried to take in what Carla had just said, but it wasn't making sense. Thirty-something, slim and athletic, Brad had just gotten his dream job, moved to a new city, and started dating a woman he had described as 'maybe The One.' His life, after several years of struggling to find his footing, was all falling into place. Of course, Carla had been saying lately that she was worried about him. She had gone to see him several*

weeks before he moved and taken him out to dinner.

"We had to stop on the way back to his apartment so he could throw up on the side of the road. He didn't have that much to drink. I think something's really wrong," she had told Emily later.

Knowing that Carla was inclined toward fatalism, Emily had pooh-poohed her fears. Brad was young, strong. Modern medicine takes care of these things. Young people get better, live long lives. It couldn't be something really bad, let alone fatal. It couldn't. But here it was. Oh Shit!

Carla had a choice here. She could have bottled up her anger, fear and depression, channeled Pollyanna, (a form of denial), and insisted it would all eventually work out fine. This approach prevents important questions from being answered and key decisions being made before it's too late. She could have carried on with a forced smile, pretending that nothing is wrong, a head-in-the-sand approach that is both emotionally and physically draining to maintain. OR, she could choose to face this scary, heartbreaking development head on and take a proactive approach in collaboration with her son. Which she – and he – did.

What matters is how you manage, together, to walk through this. A proactive, practical yet sensitive approach makes this really tough journey just a little easier and offers a better outcome for everyone involved.

WHAT IS A PROACTIVE APPROACH?

For a caregiver and the diagnosed person it starts with coming to terms with the information you've been given and making a plan. Hoping for the best in case the doctor is wrong or in case you are the single lucky soul on earth, who is never going to die, is not a plan. Realistically assessing your situation, making decisions and taking steps to be sure those decisions are well-implemented, is.

One part of the proactive approach *can* be calling friends and family, which is what Carla and Brad did. This informs everyone most closely involved, and can provide emotional support for your loved one and for you as caregiver. For many people, telling others helps. You may tell a few close friends, family, lawyer, accountant, priest/minister/rabbi/imam, or everyone and anyone who will listen. (It can actually be very helpful to tell strangers, who can be not only sympathetic but sometimes offer emotional support and perhaps a little helpful guidance with no strings and no worry about over-sharing along with over-sharing's possible repercussions. And, the compassion that strangers can offer each other makes us all feel less alone in life.). Sharing the diagnosis can help ease the emotional burden and has the added benefit of allowing you and your loved one to ask for help – from organizations, friends, family, neighbors, in short, pretty much anyone who's willing to lend a hand – and for those around you to offer it freely. (It's often surprising who will – and who won't – help). Whether large or small, loose-knit or carefully organized, this network can offer crucial support for both of you. Just as important, it offers others the opportunity to play a useful part and lets them feel needed instead of shut out. It helps to keep you and your loved one connected to a wider world and can foster bonds that will buoy both of you while offering emotional and spiritual benefits for those who have had a hand in the care.

However, others may legitimately want to keep the diagnosis private, at least for a while.

Keeping the diagnosis private, which is *not* the same as head-in-the-sand denial, can give you a little breathing space, particularly if you are reserved people. Not telling people forestalls the "How're you doing?" litany that well-intentioned friends and neighbors can play in a continuous loop, necessitating A) a continuous loop of response from you, which can be debilitating, and B) a continuous reminder that the person may be leaving soon, which can keep you both in perpetual-mourning-mode and make it more difficult to live life as well and as happily as possible day to day.

Keeping the diagnosis private does not mean that you are not taking a proactive approach. You can be taking a proactive course of action, working to stay alive and well and engaged, without telling anyone. However, this privacy can also isolate both of you, since it forces you to protect a secret, which often adds its own complexity to life.

Whichever way you chose to go is tied up in a number of things including whether sharing the information would prematurely cost someone a job (Brad's employer, who he told early on, was supportive), whether there are small children or others who may need some protection for a while, whether there will be over-the-top emotional repercussions from emotional people in your lives, and whether there are legitimate financial and insurance issues that would be unnecessarily negatively affected. The choice to share or not is primarily dependent on the personalities and circumstances of the people most closely involved.

Either way, coming to a decision about whether you will share this with no one, with trusted friends, or with all and sundry is better if it's a shared decision that both agree to.

Emily and Carla had been friends for years, so when Carla phoned, Emily insisted on coming with her.

"I told her she shouldn't be driving," Emily says now. "But she wouldn't let me. She wanted to be alone with Brad. And I understood that, but I was still worried that she might have an accident on the way. It was a long drive, but I knew I could only push her so far before I turned into a problem instead of a help.

"So when she came, I just held her and we cried. I was still thinking that a positive outlook helps a lot and wanted to give her hope, so she could give it to Brad, so when we both stopped crying, I said, something like: "Maybe it will be OK. They can do so much now."

"You know what she said?" Emily continued. "She said, 'I've already had a vision of burying my son." I was shocked! I thought: she's already given up. But I didn't say that, of course. In fact, I said almost nothing. She just wanted to talk and get calmer before she took that long drive to face what the two of them were going to have to go through together. It was awful. I knew, once she'd said what she did, that there was nothing I could say that was going to help. All I could really do was listen."

If you're part of the support system for either the person diagnosed or the loved one who will offer care, your job is to support without pushiness or criticism, which can only add to the burden those closest are carrying. Support can come in many forms. (More about this later.)

When you first learn of the diagnosis, particularly if you are going to be the primary caregiver, your first reaction could easily be: I can't! I can't cope, live without them, survive this, do this! Why me?! Why us? You want to kick something, cry, bash something, scream, throw a world-class tantrum.

Do it. Let it out.

If you live in an apartment or place where the neighbors will call the police when you start doing this, find another way – a physical way – yanking weeds, power walking, a punching bag at the gym, punching pillows at home, shooting hoops, biking, dancing, splitting wood, going out to the remotest field you can find and screaming until you're hoarse, whatever – to drain this initial flood of emotion from your body. Exhaust yourself physically then sleep.

If you're going to be primary caregiver, this could be the most overwhelming job of your life. Life has thrust this role on you, usually with little time to prepare. You may feel resentful, frantic, stuck. You may even exit, either emotionally or physically, for a short time to get your mind around what you fear is up ahead. (Once Brad was safely through the first surgery, Carla took off and spent two days alone at the beach staring out to sea.).

There is nothing comfortable about this. Having acknowledged that isn't easy it's also important to know that there can be incomparable rewards. (Carla and Brad talked intimately, seriously, hilariously throughout the whole process, a gift to each of them.).

NOW, BREATHE DEEPLY

You can't control circumstances, but you can control what you do about them, how you react. Okay, before you throw this book across the room, try not to say, 'I can't'; say 'I'll try.' And then start to think about the new reality.

DOCTORS DON'T HAVE THE CALENDAR

One of the first questions people usually ask after a terminal diagnosis is: How long do we have? The answer you get depends on several things: on the person diagnosed; on the disease and their condition; on their physical and financial circumstances; and on their own determination. The answer you get also depends on the physician. Some physicians will offer a timeline, a general guess that may help to push the person and their nearest and dearest into getting things in order instead of putting off crucial decisions and practical steps until it's too late. Other doctors will shrug and say they don't know. Still others will say it all depends on a host of factors, including the person's general health and will to live; they may offer a time frame that spans weeks to years. Whichever way the physician choses to play it – offer hope by saying they don't know, or offer a timeline, which feels like a countdown to a death sentence – it's important to remember that doctors don't have the calendar on another person's life. They work from what they have seen, from what others have shared with them, and what current research indicates (or at least the research your individual physician is aware of). But there is no expiration date written on the bottoms of our feet – or anywhere else, for that matter.

Some years ago, Nancy had a friend who had been diagnosed with Stage 4 liver cancer. Barbara had been told she only four months to live. Her initial response to the Oh Shit Moment was to shut down her life completely. The fear and shock of what might be ahead paralyzed her. When Nancy went to see her, she found Barbara, a retired teacher, stuck in the house, unable to force herself to do any of the things that until then had given her pleasure and purpose. Seeing friends, going to church, even eating seemed worthless. 'What's the point if I'll be gone by Christmas?" she demanded.

Although Barbara was both a faithful churchgoer and a woman of faith (which is not always the same thing), the diagnosis had knocked her flat. The Biblical platitudes – It's God's will, He wouldn't give you more to bear than you could stand, You'll be in a better place – that churchgoers sometimes offer in an effort to comfort – were zero help.

(In fact, they often make even fellow churchgoers want to slap the speaker).

Nancy's initial response was pragmatic: You still have to eat, let me take you to lunch. Although Barbara resisted at first — one of the symptoms of the cancer had been difficulty with digestion — Barbara allowed herself to be taken out to a local lunchroom. And with the change in scenery, she was able to work her way through most of a bowl of chicken noodle soup as well as frank conversation about how the diagnosis and the way the doctor had delivered the news had affected her outlook. It helped a little. Additionally, getting off the sofa and out of the house was a simple step that prodded Barbara to re-open the door to what life was left for her — which turned out to be not four months, but four more years!

"They keep asking me to come take more tests, since they can't figure out why I'm still here," she laughed not long before she died.

TIP: Regardless of timeline, once a person receives a terminal diagnosis, it's important to be sure their affairs are in order and if not, to urge them to get them in order. If they put it off until too late, they condemn their nearest and dearest not only the grief of their loss, but the significant burden — and resulting resentment — of sorting out whatever financial, physical and emotional debris they've left behind.

CURE VERSUS CARE

While some cultures and many religions teach that death is a blessing because the person's spirit is going home, our DNA urges us to stay alive in our physical bodies any way we can. The US culture's own never-say-die attitude seduces us into thinking we actually *can* live forever provided we take good enough care of ourselves, do yoga, practice clean living, take vitamins, and nip and tuck and replacement-part our way to perpetual youth — which makes a terminal diagnosis especially hard to accept, for doctors as well as patients. Eat right, exercise, die anyway. (Just maybe a little later than you might have otherwise).

"What do we really know about death and how do we approach it?" one primary care physician asks rhetorically.

Doctors are taught to identify symptoms, alleviate pain and suffering and to try to cure. For some doctors, particularly specialists, end-stage palliative care can represent failure.

In addition, our society demands that every attempt, however unrealistic or futile, be made to *cure* the person. We think: Maybe it's terminal, then again, maybe it's not - yet. What else can we try? As a result, both doctors and the person's loved ones must 'prove' that all medical options have been exhausted before considering end-stage palliative care, an approach that can lead not only to unnecessary, potentially painful, and often expensive procedures that may or may not prolong life, but that can have a huge impact on the quality of the time remaining.

In some cases, doctors feel pressured to keep performing more procedures and tests – a safeguard against potential liability suits brought by frustrated, grief-stricken family members, and usually also born of a sense of duty – waiting until the last possible moment to prescribe palliative care or to refer a dying person to hospice care. By that time, steps may have already been taken that make shifting from cure mode to comfort mode and to the inevitable letting go not just emotionally complicated but legally complicated; the family may need to fight to unhook the person from a host of machines. If the person is to be discharged from a hospital to hospice care, whether at home or in a facility, there are criteria for Medicare reimbursements, which, as we write this, are in flux.

"[Currently] the hospice benefit requires the physician to say that the patient is going to live less than six months," says Dr. Helen Noble, a primary care physician. "In agreeing to the benefit, a patient agrees to forgo further treatment in the hospital that may be life-prolonging."

By calling in hospice, you give up your right to go to the hospital to get life-prolonging care, (though it does not preclude orders to attempt resuscitation should a patient's heart stop). Having already said that doctors don't have a calendar, we must understand that doctors are making educated guesses.

"It's sometimes so difficult to be able to distinguish between someone who is severely ill but has the potential to recover or improve," says Dr. Noble, "and someone who is at the end of life. With cancer it's sometimes apparent when there's nothing more that can be done, but not always; with other kinds of illness – heart disease, dementia – decline and demise are often fairly unpredictable."

But not always.

Complicating the decision-making is the family. Sometimes they are inconsistent – or worse, in conflict with each other – when discussing the person's wishes with the doctor (which is where a Living Will and Medical Directive come in – more about this later). One grown child may be certain it's time to move to palliative care, while another may insist that Mom or Dad has more time if the hospital or doctor would just do *one more thing*. Or the dying person and their family may be in denial, so when a doctor says he or she has done all they can, the family feels abandoned.

"People have to go through a process before they get to being ready to accept hospice, and sometimes that process is straightforward and pretty easy, while sometimes it's so difficult with people wanting to hang onto their lives, responsibilities, loved ones," says Dr. Noble. "Sometimes it takes weeks and months of the patient and their family seeing it one way and the doctor seeing it another. Sometimes it's the opposite. It's not [just] numbers and lab tests that you have to be tuned into."

One patient, a long-time smoker and cancer sufferer who had already undergone numerous procedures over the years, was actually in the end stages of her life.

"She had a very strong will to live and was always looking for one more reason to hope," says Noble.

She was having trouble breathing and came back to the doctor, expecting to be put into the hospital for one more procedure, one more 'cure' or at least something to buy her more time. But the doctor could see that there was nothing more to be done except possibly to make the patient more comfortable.

"The [good] doctor is always asking his or herself: Is this intervention going to make a difference," says Noble. "It's a way of practicing economy, not directing resources where they're not going to make a difference. Society is in the midst of tremendous policy shifts and changes in the way we deliver medical care, and it's because of our demographics and our economy."

With this particular patient, the doctor initiated a conversation about hospice.

"The son, who was very devoted all along, was there, and I could see that he got it," she says. "But his mother was still in denial. I sent her home with some [palliative medication], and phoned hospice, asking that they go see her."

But when the hospice workers went to the house, the woman turned them away.

"I thought about it for a while," says the doctor. "What's my responsibility here? I called hospice again, and asked that they try again, but this time, I said to talk with the son. This time, they were accepted. They came to her home, and she died 24 hours later. I knew it was close, but I didn't expect that!"

Did the woman finally acquiesce to the inevitable? Or did her body? Or both? We don't know.

"To me," Noble says, "the looming issue is: When and how are you going to die? How are you going to wrap up your life [well] if you won't allow yourself the opportunity to acknowledge what's happening?"

Often, in a long-term terminal patient, once the specialist has done everything, they tend to absent themselves when the person has reached the palliative care stage.

"There are some specialists who tend to get hands-off at the end stages and turn the patient back to their primary care physician," says Noble. "In some it's denial of personal feeling, of not wanting to be close to [the impending death], and for some it's a sense of 'not my job.' I admire those who recognize that they have a long-term relationship with the person, and with that, a responsibility to help this person to live and die with their serious illness," she says.

Doctors don't like death any more than the rest of us (probably less since it constitutes a failure on their part to cure or at least prolong healthy life). And while they are taught to be clinical, detached, or may be that way naturally, there are times when a doctor's emotions can overwhelm their professional demeanor.

Mother's Day at the hospice center. The 36-year-old weekend doctor was making her rounds. When Sue walked into the nurse's station, she found the doctor sitting in a chair quietly crying. Sue stood, taken aback for a moment, then walked over and put her arm around the doctor's shoulder. The doctor leaned her head into Sue's side and began to sob.

"Who did you visit?" Sue asked.

"The young woman down the hall with the cervical cancer," she said, sobbing louder. "I have failed! I've failed!"

The doctor's visit to the woman had prompted the outburst. When the doctor went into the room, the patient's seventeen-year-old son had been sitting alone by his mother's bedside and had asked the doctor the Holy Grail of questions: How long? The young doctor's sudden image of her own five-year-son, who was at home with his father this Mother's Day, in searing contrast to the Mother's Day this boy was having, shattered her professional detachment.

"I could not answer him," she cried. "I could feel the tears coming, and if I opened my mouth I would have lost it in front of him. I've failed this boy greatly."

"You're human," Sue told her gently. "It's okay to cry in front of patients and families, as long as you don't make your crying their burden."

"I can't go back into that room and look at him or I will loose it, but I can't ignore him. I don't know what to do," the doctor insisted miserably.

"After you gain your composure, go back and tell him you're sorry for leaving abruptly, that you got a little emotional and had to step out," Sue advised.

But in the end, the doctor, who believed she would burst into tears at the sight of this woman's son, couldn't bring herself to return. Another nurse spoke with him instead.

TELL THE CHILDREN

In some circumstances, particularly when the terminal diagnosis is for a parent with young children, people are inclined to keep the truth a secret.

It's done out of an understandable effort to protect the children as long as possible. It can take the form of saying little, or by denying what is happening when the children ask questions – because in all likelihood they will – or in outright lying to them with assurances that 'Mommy will get better.' The problem is, children almost always sense when something is going on in their family's lives. In the absence of some kind of honesty in addressing the situation, children will dive into their own little reptilian brains and come up with their own potentially skewed and self-blaming explanations for the tension in the house. Many will convince themselves that Mommy or Daddy got sick because they were bad, or did something they shouldn't have for which the parent's illness is punishment. This is worse than the truth, which is already awful enough.

Mary, one of Sue's friends and co-workers, was diagnosed several years ago with thyroid cancer, which is often curable. Of course she and her husband were worried, but they tried to keep their worries from their children, letting them know about the diagnosis, but downplaying it considerably in an effort to keep everything in their lives 'normal.' Yet she and her husband would consult in low voices when they thought the children were out of earshot. Later, she learned that one of her sons had resented the secrecy. She explained that she had been keeping it secret in an effort to keep everything normal. It hadn't worked. The son's response: 'Nothing in this house was NORMAL!'

"I can tell you that in the time alone that kid is gonna fill his mind with horror stories about the most horrible stuff he thinks is going to be happening," says Ben Brack, who was nine when his mother was diagnosed with cancer. "To have access to the reality – 'Yeah, this is scary, and we're gonna live through it until we don't, and this is part of The Plan' [helps]. It's inclusion. I think it was a good thing [my mom's diagnosis] wasn't pushed behind my parents' bedroom door and locked."

BUT you don't need to smack the children between the eyes with all the details, either.

So, how should you deal with them? In a word: honestly, but with an eye to their age and their ability to comprehend what you're saying. You don't want the child to think Mommy or Daddy's (or Grandmom's or Uncle Homer's) illness is somehow their fault. Or that it's contagious, as some children believe with things like cancer. You also don't want them to grow up and one day tell you they will never forgive you for keeping things from them, for blocking their chance to say goodbye (as that seventeen-year-old son had the opportunity – and made the choice – to do). You don't want to tell them that their parent or grandparent or friend 'left' so they think they've been abandoned and will spend their lives hoping that someday they may come back! Without honesty, the children could harbor regrets and resentments that can never be resolved once the person is gone.

Yet being honest is very tough to balance against the need to protect children from unnecessary pain. Honesty needs to be tempered with an understanding of both their age and their individual readiness to hear what's happening. It takes thought, perception, and a little exploration of the individual child.

Children are just as individual as adults. A one-year-old could have a full head of hair, teeth, be walking and talking with ease while another could be a cue ball and still getting around on all fours at two. Sue's friends gave her joke gift certificates for a hair weave and dentures for her son's first birthday. He was walking and talking fine, but only had spuds of hair on top of his head and two teeth. Her pediatrician told her not to worry, by the time they get to kindergarten they pretty much look the same, he told her, they just get there in their own time. Children's emotional and coping abilities develop in their own time as well, depending in part on their individual temperaments and in part on the home environment. So how and when to tell a child about the impending death of a loved one, particularly the impeding death of a parent, truly depends on the child.

Talk to them. Listen carefully to what they say; pay attention to the questions they ask. That will give you a little insight into how they perceive what's happening and give you guidance on what to say.

If the person is a grandparent or lives elsewhere, there may be time lapses between visits during which there may be a big change in the person's appearance. You can explain that grandma or Uncle Joe is very sick, that she or he might look different, may even look scary (if features are gaunt). Prepare the child for the visit without freaking them out. Then give the child the choice. Ask the child if they want to see the person.

Nancy's then eight- and ten-year-old children went with her to her father's house every day to see their beloved 'Pop,' as he lay dying for several weeks. Finally, after one visit, eight-year-old Abby told her mother, "I don't wanna go any more. I'm afraid he'll die while I'm there, and I don't want to see it."

Honoring her child's clearly stated wishes, from then on when she went to see her father, Nancy left Abby with friends. Her ten-year-old son continued to come, though more, Nancy believes, to support her and keep her company on the hour-long drive than to see his grandfather, who was by then in a hospital bed in the den. Matt would lean into the room to say hello, then go off to the living room to read alone. His presence was an act of generosity and consideration for his mother, and a sign of emotional maturing. Then one day, Nancy's father was in vocal pain. It was too much for Matt, who said he didn't want to come any more, a choice Nancy not only respected but appreciated his articulating.

When her father died, Nancy was at his side, but her children were with friends having ice cream and a happy day on the river, which helped to soften the blow for both the children and for Nancy. She returned home with sad news, but the kids were so excited to tell her about their day, she saved her news for them until the following day.

But losing a grandfather is not the same as losing a mom. And likely does not take place in the same home the child is in.

For two long days ten-year-old Michael watched his mother, Pam, pace the house, moaning and crying with end-stage breast cancer that had gone to her liver, which meant she was in constant pain. Finally, Michael's dad, Sam, brought Pam to the hospice center, leaving Michael with a neighbor.

When Pam arrived at the hospice center, it was clear she was very close to death. At one point her color turned to clay, the area around her mouth became bluish, her lips colorless and her eyes started to roll back into her head. Sue immediately put a hand on her chest, rubbed it in a circle and leaned in near her ear.

"Pam. I am going to have Sam call the children, will you wait for them?" Sue asked. Pam couldn't answer.

Pam had three children from a previous marriage in addition to Michael. Michael's father was concerned that he was too young to witness his mother in such a state, but Sue suggested that he put the question to Michael instead of making the decision for him. After all, the boy had spent all weekend with her at home in obvious pain.

Sam agreed, but when Michael approached his mother's room and heard her moaning, he halted at the door. After a second, he turned around, sat down on the chair in the hallway and drew himself up onto a ball, face hidden on his knees. Sue gently asked him if he wanted her to take him into the room. He shook his buried head. No. Would you like to go to the toy room? Again he shook his head. No.

Later, Sue walked by Pam's room, and noticed the empty chair in the hall. She peeked inside and saw Pam's other three children from her first marriage, all in late teens and early twenties. Michael was snuggled on the lap of his eldest half-sister, who was rocking him. He had made the choice to be there. When his mother died, Michael was wrapped in quiet, loving support with the rest of his family instead of being isolated outside the room.

Despite our efforts to reduce life to a series of predictable steps and easily categorized criteria, for so much of our lives we're feeling our way along an unfamiliar path ourselves, which can make it that much more difficult to discern how best to deal with children about to lose someone very close to them. Yet it's so much better to at least try to give them an option in these situations rather than pretend nothing is happening. Mary remembered her son's anger at being kept in the dark when she was working through thyroid cancer, so when she was later diagnosed with pancreatic cancer, she sat down and told each child individually.

Some children want and need to be protected until they can't be protected any longer. Others need to be included. It's a soup-to-nuts mix; whether or not to tell a child depends on a host of factors including the personalities involved, the ages of the children, and the circumstances.

Sue, who was fourteen when her grandmother died, had not been told the seriousness of her grandmother's illness.

"I felt blindsided [when they told me she died]," she says now. "I wasn't given any explanation. The death came out of the blue, and I found myself sitting in the church beside the casket, sobbing uncontrollably, and I'm not even really sure why I was sobbing; it was all so strange."

In contrast, Rachel Gillotti, who lost her father when she was eleven, was not shielded from the facts. The poem she wrote only months after his death illustrates a surprisingly mature strength and understanding. It is also a reminder that adults should not automatically shut children out; it's better to give them the choice about whether to be present.

I'll GET OVER IT
by
Rachel Gillotti

Life isn't fair
Things happen that I can not control
Things of horror, depression and hurt
I wish I could stop them, destroy them
I want to control them, but I'll get over it
People are hurt every day
Loved ones lost
Depression deepens as the hurt sets in
Like a cut so very deep but I'll get over it
Funerals start the caskets are carried
While they await the dark moment
Prayers are said
Songs are done
Now we bury the casket
But I'll get over it
Grim faces like a dark dreary night
Await me at the door, saying their goodbyes
One last chance to say my prayers
And then I must leave but I'll get over it
I am sad

I am depressed
I am sorrowful
But I'll get over it
I *will* get over it
I will build a bridge and get over it
I will stop being sad
I will be the best person I can be
Depression won't hurt me
I'll get over it.

No one can know exactly what it feels like to a parent to leave young children behind, though it has to be agonizing, a sense of leaving the most important mission of your life unfinished. But if we can't prevent it, we can help the dying leave a loving legacy behind, a little hand-beyond-the-grave contact.

CAREGIVER/LOVED ONE TIP: Help the dying person fill out greeting cards for their child's (or grandchild's in the case of a grandparent with a close relationship with the child) milestone occasions such as reaching benchmark ages or graduating from grade school, high school or college. Attach a letter or letters that offer 'words of wisdom' about any of life's experiences — learning to drive a car, play an instrument, play a sport, or attending their first dance, surviving their first love, getting married, having children. The cards can pass on family traditions, recipes, heritage, history, family or cultural lore and more. Make molds of the hands of the dying for a child or grandchildren.

Writing a journal can be helpful for the dying person and others. Pat Brack wrote Moms Don't get Sick *(Melius Publishing Corp. 1990) with her youngest child, Ben, when she was diagnosed with breast cancer. Brack, a teacher and administrator at a private school in Baltimore, gave her three sons as much information as she felt they could handle, but could see that her youngest, Ben, then ten years old, was feeling scared and isolated.*

She was looking for ways to help him when Ben suggested that the two of them write a book together, a project that turned out to be joint therapy. In alternating pages Ben wrote about what he was feeling at a given time or about a specific situation, and then Pat wrote a page about it. As a result, the book offers both a mother's and a child's eye view of the effect the illness had on each of them as well as the whole family.

"Having a parent become seriously ill causes unexpected change and confusion in a family," she said.

"I realized how important mothers are when my mom got cancer," Ben said at fourteen when the book was published. "Thinking my mom might die was the worst thing that every happened to me."

*The writing itself as well as the conversations it sparked and the feelings it opened up helped both Pat and Ben process and cope with her diagnosis. **

"Writing the book, the process was helpful," Ben Brack says now. "You've got a young kid talking about his perspective on what was going on and you're actually listening to what a child has to say, and to be listened to was huge."

However, he views the subsequent publicity surrounding the book's publication differently.

"This was Mom's swansong and I was a large part of that, so I got swept away," he says. "I was fifteen or sixteen and awkward. Going on 'cancer rally tours' with my mom is not the usual fifteen to sixteen-year-old-boy agenda – and I was a little pissed off. But it gave me a background in public speaking that I use now."

Brack says one thing he might change was to keep private the journal the two did together.

"A family doesn't need to make a major statement with a life," he says. "If it's done as: "Hey this is our family history and it was a good one – make a scrap book.""

*Pat lost her battle in 1995 when Ben was 20.

WHAT ABOUT ADULT CHILDREN?

As children grow into adulthood, the relationship between parent and child usually morphs into something like friendship. Roles may even reverse if the parent needs support of any kind. Yet even with this more adult relationship, however loving and mature, there is usually enough emotional baggage to take everyone to Timbuktu and back again, baggage that can complicate the decision-making process. As a result, facing the inevitable and putting things in order while there is still time can be an emotional minefield. A parent may feel the need to withhold critical health and financial information from a grown child. Some parents still view themselves as mentors and want to protect the grown child, who, they believe, 'can't handle the truth.' (Their grown children may feel the same way about the parents). Some parents withhold information for fear that the adult children will take over their lives entirely and steamroll decisions the parent may not agree with. This push-me-pull-you relationship, whether acknowledged or not can create all kinds of stress on both sides.

Yet living with a gnawing sense that something's wrong, that something critical in a parent's health has changed, but getting no enlightenment from the parent can leave adult children feeling shut out, worried and resentful – to say nothing of feeling utterly helpless in a situation that will most likely deeply involve them later if not sooner.

"For the loving adult child, it's a jaw-breaker-sized pill to swallow when the parent refuses to let you in," says Sue, who speaks from experience. "Hospice nurses call this reluctance to come clean about what's going on *The Mom Syndrome*, but Dads can exhibit it too."

The months that led to Sue's father's death in 2000 offered plenty of evidence that he was NOT OK. His pasty grey color, his struggle to breathe, and his gaspy voice, all told the nurse in Sue that there was a change – and not a good one.

"I had sensed this during the several months leading up to his death," she remembers. "I even asked my cousin, a cardiac nurse, to pay him a visit to get her take on what I was feeling."

Attempting to help, Sue also offered her dad plenty of advice – install an air conditioner during the city's steamy summer heat, get a portable oxygen canister and get medication to help with breathing – all of which he rejected saying he already had a doctor and therefore didn't need her input.

"You don't tell the doctor what to do," he told her, despite her nursing credentials.

He also insisted on cutting his own grass, a job that could have easily killed him. Sue knew instinctively that something was off, but was unable to penetrate her father's protective armor.

"I was sitting with my daughter when he called on Sunday evening," Sue remembers.

Her daughter, Sarah, was a new vegetarian, who had given her grandfather some nutritional advice.

"Tell Sarah she was right about the diet," her father rasped into the phone.

"His tone was different," Sue says now. "He must have sensed my thoughts because he went into his usual rhetoric about the government, the banks, and the decline of the country. The conversation was short. I remember commenting to Sarah that something seemed off, and that I should call him back, but she stopped me."

"He'll give you a hard time if you call him back," she said.

Sue heeded her daughter's advice, but slept badly, troubled on and off during the night. He died at home that night. They found him two days later.

"When I called his doctor to request a signature on a death certificate," Sue says, "his doctor said he was a 'miracle man.'"

Stunned by his death, Sue didn't stop to ask what the doctor had meant by that. She learned later that her father had known for about a year that he had limited time. The recent numbers on his heart's ejection fraction (a measurement of volume of blood leaving the heart with each contraction) meant he was not a transplant candidate. Her nurse cousin had known, but was bound by patient confidentiality to keep it secret. It hurt Sue deeply that her father had refused to confide in her – perhaps to protect her or protect himself from Sue's "shoulding on him" as in: 'Dad, you should...' Yet even with her own hurt and frustration at his refusal to let her help, Sue felt as though he was at peace. He lived – and died – as he wanted, something Sue is smart enough – and practical enough – to know she will want for herself one day.

Resources for Telling The Children:

The Kid's Book About Death and Dying by Eric Rofes

Water Bugs and Dragonflies: Explaining Death to Young Children by Doris Stickney illustrated by Gloria Claudia Ortiz

Because . . . Someone I Love Has Cancer: Kids' Activity Book [Spiral-Bound] American Cancer Society (Author)

Talking about Death: A Dialogue Between Parent and Child by Earl A. Grollman

Moms Don't Get Sick by Pat Brack and Ben Brack

Chapter Two

OKAY NOW WHAT?

Now that you've heard the diagnosis, particularly if you're going to be the primary caregiver, there's a slew of questions – financial, physical and emotional – cascading through your mind. Your responsibility for and control over both the questions and answers will probably depend on the relationship you have with the person as well as the person him or herself.

There was a time not long ago, when birth and death took place at home, so both were a matter of common conversation and common experience. Today, new technology has removed many of us from close contact with end-of-life realities and from open acknowledgement about this crucial life event. Death is a downer; it's impolite even to bring up the subject. But shrouding what's happening in silence doesn't prevent a terminal illness from progressing or prevent death from eventually coming. Poet Emily Dickenson had it right when she wrote: *Because I could not stop for Death, He kindly stopped for me;.*

IT'S STILL THEIR LIFE

The first thing to do, especially if you're going to be the fulltime caregiver and are going to take the proactive approach, is to start with the person. This may or may not be a head-on soup-to-nuts discussion. More likely, you and the person will tackle the answers to some of the critical questions in bits and pieces as opportunity, emotion and time allow. Carla says she never *really* discussed much with her son, Brad, following the diagnosis.

"I went to the doctors with him, and listened to the surgeon," she remembers. "Sometimes I'd ask for a clarification. But we never really discussed what he would do. I was available to him. I went to the hospital, took care of him when he needed me to, but it was his life, and he was the one who needed to choose how to play it."

You may be feeling resentment at where their and your life is going at this point. You may even feel as though they have brought themselves to this earlier-than-hoped-for pass exactly because of the way they have lived up to this point and hope that this will be the wake-up call that inspires them to make a radical change. Take a breath and try to relax. It isn't going to happen. And you aren't going to make it happen. You can't change a person who doesn't want to change, and it's debilitating and exhausting for all involved to try. (You can, however, sometimes, influence, gently).

You may well be reluctant to initiate a conversation about how they envision this journey. They may be reluctant, too. But it's important to try. Decisions need to be made.

Are they willing to talk about what's coming and what needs to be done in preparation or do they clam up? Perhaps they begin by referring to death obliquely, for example, talking about when a parent, a loved one or friend died, musing about that person's funeral arrangements or lack of them. You may need to start by approaching the questions sideways instead of head on, drawing clues and potential openings from their conversation. For example, if they bring up Aunt Maude's incredibly over-the-top funeral (or beautifully done funeral, depending on their bent), listen carefully. Rather than give your opinion, ask what they thought about it and why. They may offer something along the lines of: 'She always was a show-off; I never liked that about her.' Or conversely, 'Well, it was over-the-top, but it's something that no one will ever forget.' Either way, it offers an opportunity to begin a discussion about whether or not they have something in mind for themselves.

If so, it's also a good idea for the person to record it in some way – write it down, video it, tape record it, whatever – and let the people who will most likely be dealing with it know where they can find the person's record. We've seen more than one family argue bitterly over the funeral, only to stumble much later upon a handwritten notation about what the deceased wanted following their demise. Having recorded in some tangible way and letting it be known where that record can be found saves SO many arguments about the immediate steps following the loved one's death, whether the arguments are philosophical, religious or economic.

Nancy's mother, a Christian Scientist, had always stated – and eventually wrote in her will – that she wanted to be cremated. However, she was silent on the subject of funeral or memorial services. In the Christian Science Church, there are no rites for the dead. As a result, Nancy's mother's ashes sat on her father's mantelpiece in the box they were delivered in (with the tag and invoice copy still attached!) for a year. When her father was about to marry a second time, Nancy and her brother decided it was not a good idea to leave them there. So, she, her brother and father privately buried her mother's ashes in a spot of ground her mother had always loved and said a prayer over it, knowing that they had done both a loving and respectful thing for the person that their mother and wife was.

When her father died, he too was cremated (as per his written wishes) but for him, they held a big Episcopal church service with a cast of thousands followed by a raucus wake with an open bar and music provided by her father's musician buddies. Which was fitting for the person that he was.

This is also a good time for you to consider whether or not you have something written down for your own last rites, if you want any, since any of us could be hit by a bus with little warning but the last-minute BEEP!

Having these kinds of personal conversations with someone who has had a terminal diagnosis is rarely easy, especially initially. Sometimes, it's virtually impossible if they resist too strenuously. They may be resisting coming to terms with this diagnosis, but it's also possible that they may not want to have these conversations *with you*, yet may be open to talking this kind of thing over with someone less intimately involved – a pastor, rabbi, trusted friend or relation. Recognizing when someone is obliquely initiating a conversation about their own demise takes perception. Gently urging it to a result takes both courage and a deft touch because it forces both of you to face the reality of our own ends, including the rat's nest of fear, anger and sadness that can overwhelm us at such a parting. Even though conversations about the approaching leave-taking can be very difficult, a tenderly honest approach can not only resolve crucial practical issues, it can also lead to sharing stories, memories, ideas, and laughter, which help to strengthen bonds and sustain both cared-for and caregiver.

It's important to remember too, that having conversations that help put things in place for the inevitable departure does not need to squash hope for a longer active life than the medical community may have predicted. Like Barbara, who was advised to do everything she needed to do before Christmas the year she was pronounced terminal, your loved one may be getting called back to research labs fours years after the terminal diagnosis to find out why they're still alive.

BUT *counting* on a much-longer timeline is not only unwise; it's selfish. It's the I-Can't-Be-Out-of-Time-I-Still-Have-Stuff-to-Do syndrome (akin to the I-Can't-Be-Out-Of-Money-I-Still-Have-Checks/a Debit-Card Syndrome, which plays havoc with budgets). That denial, or if you prefer, refusal to acknowledge even the possibility of death, only shoves everything under the carpet where it remains lumpy and awkward; it doesn't eliminate it. Paperwork needs to be in place, decisions that are best made by the person, or at least with the person's input, need to be resolved and acted upon. Refusing to deal pragmatically with what's coming can leave a huge mess behind, producing a fair amount of resentment and hard work in addition to the grief for those who must deal with it. The initial shock of the terminal diagnosis, which knocked Barbara flat at first, was the time during which she took care of a lot of business that helped make things much easier for her family when she eventually died.

In Carla's son's case, Brad wrote out a will and gave his mother the documented power to make medical decisions for him should that be necessary. He simply went to a lawyer and had the necessary legal papers drawn up, witnessed and signed, then told Carla what he had done and showed her where they were kept. Carla accepted his statement and left it at that. A practical, though potentially wrenching chore taken care of with minimal fuss and anguish. And then he went on to fight for his life with every fiber.

The conversation about this kind of thing does not need to be long, involved and filled with wailing. It can be very simple and short. You don't want to traipse all over the person's personal business. They may want it all to be very private for legitimate reasons that they don't wish to discuss. You just want to be sure the person is informed about what needs to be in place (provided of course they are in control of their faculties, which is another can of worms). One thing that helps to prod people into putting the paperwork in place is to remind them that if they do not make their wishes known officially, someone else – likely a state or county bureaucrat, who may or may not make them in accordance with the person's undocumented but fervent wishes – will in all likelihood be deciding things for them and for those they leave behind.

None of this has to be decided immediately (unless there is reason to believe that the time is very short indeed), but it's helpful, particularly in the case of blended families, which can add to already fraught emotions and differences of tradition and outlook, to have it all nailed down legally while the person is still in charge of his or her own life, and to let the people around you know where those documents are. It's also no good having it stuck at the back of the sock drawer where the family won't find out that their loved one wanted cremation until after they've paid for embalming and an expensive casket.

DON'T FORGET ONLINE ACCOUNTS. Now that so much of our lives, both personal and financial, takes place on the internet or electronically, it is also a good idea for the person to be sure to leave instructions on how to access online accounts of all kinds. One friend took his own life not long ago. He had been responsible for an incapacitated sister and had done all of both his and his sibling's banking and financial transactions online. There was no paper trail for his grief-stricken remaining brother to follow when trying to unravel the threads of Gregg's life, settle his affairs and take care of their sister. As a result, for months after Gregg's sudden death, his brother was using his own already over-burdened credit cards to pay bills while he struggled to maintain his own life and work, take care of his sister and find the location and passwords to online accounts.

PAPERWORK AND PRACTICALITIES

Below are the documents that need to be put in place.

1. **Power of Attorney** (POA) gives a designated agent (hopefully a trustworthy person) the authority to act on financial or legal matters. It allows someone other than (usually in addition to) the dying person to sign checks, pay bills, and conduct banking and other business on behalf of the person. It can be broad (a general POA) or limited. This document dies with the person.

2. **Medical Power of Attorney or 'Health Care Agent"** gives a specified person or persons the power to make health care decisions.

3. **Living Will** specifies the person's wishes regarding extreme medical measures to prolong life (or not). It helps to give copies to the doctor, the hospital and any other health care agent early in the process.

4. **H**ealth **I**nsurance **P**ortability and **A**ccountability **A**ct of 1996 (**HIPAA**) Privacy and Security Rules authorizes a specified person (usually the caregiver and/or family members) to ask for and receive information concerning health issues; it allows the doctor to share details of the patient with the designated person, who can then decide who else to share that information with. In some states, there is a form called Medical Orders for Life-Sustaining Treatment (MOLST) that, once filled in, travels with the person from facility to facility in a way that some of these other forms and directives do not. Maryland and Massachusetts are two states with MOLST forms. Other states have similar forms though with different acronyms.

If there are no such documents in place, now is the time to introduce the need for them. Unfortunately, many people fear they will be signing away their ability to change their minds or control the situation should they still be able. For those reluctant to draw up legal documents relating to what they wish should they become incapable of making choices for themselves, it's important to stress that Advanced Directives and Do Not Resuscitate orders can be rescinded; a person can change his or her mind at any time.

If there are already legal documents in place, now is the time to get them out and be sure they are up to date. Will they impact the caregiver and if so, how? Giving care without enough good information, particularly medical information, is awkward at best (possibly even dangerous, another can of worms we won't get into here). Has the person always paid all the bills and taken care of all the business for a couple? A family? A business? Now is the time for them to share information to help make transitions smoother.

To begin, sit down with a legal pad, calendar, iPad, laptop, or whatever device you choose – and will keep at hand – to write down the list of things that need to be considered. Then start checking off what is in place already and what needs to be dealt with. Be sure to include deadlines for tasks. (Two short checklists at the end of this book will help to get you started).

RALLY THE TROOPS (Unless You Plan to Keep It Private)

Once the to-do list is made, it helps to call family – family being anyone you deem to be family, blood or otherwise. This gives everyone an opportunity to participate. Give people a list of what needs to be done for the foreseeable future. As people offer to help – and they will in all likelihood – be sure to write that down, too. There will probably be a host of small details to keep track of; having it on paper or on a digital device is easier than trying to carry everything in your head. It's also more likely to get done if it's recorded in a place you check regularly – often that means the kitchen, desk or a chest of drawers.

Get in touch with friends, co-workers, members of the person's (and your) religious organization, clubs, neighborhood, community or personal network. The more people you have available to help, the less stress you will feel. Do you know someone working in health care? They may be a great resource for finding equipment, daily care or respite care and they may know, or help to chase down, how to get things covered through insurance. The primary care doctor and/or his office staff can also be good resources for this kind of information. At the end of this chapter, there is a list of organizations that can help or that can guide you to where you can find help.

CONSIDERATIONS AND COMMON WORRIES:

1. Financial:
   - Will you need to take a leave of absence from work? Is that possible? Or if you try to take a leave, will you lose your job?
   - If you take a leave, how will the bills get paid? Is there insurance? What will it cover?
   - Does the person requiring care have enough money for all of their needs and prescriptions?
   - Do they have money to give you if you take a leave of absence?
   - If the answer to both those questions is no, what resources can you and they call on to supplement?
   - Is the person the family's rock, bill-payer, and person-in-charge in addition to main financial support? Be sure that the

surviving spouse/ significant other /children's guardian learns what they need to know to carry on effectively.

-

2. Physical:
   - If you don't already live with them, will you take care of them in their home or bring them to your house?
   - Will they need someone with them around the clock or in shifts?
   - What obstacles could you face together in their physical decline?
   - Will you need to install special equipment to help them get around or help you help them?
   - Where would you be able to get supplies?
   - How much medical care might you be physically able to give? Are you dealing with your own physical issues, too?
   - What happens if they cannot walk to the bathroom?
   - Could you change a diaper on an adult who cannot assist you? (The prospect of this can be daunting to most of us). Is there help so you don't have to do it? If not, will you get accustomed to it? (It's surprising how accustomed one can get to things we didn't think we could cope with).
   - What if they suddenly have difficulty breathing?
   - What if they get congested and can no longer cough?
   - What about giving medication or narcotics?
   - What if they insist you give them a larger dose than the one prescribed?
   - What if they beg for an overdose?
   - How do you know when the pain is controlled?
   - What if they decide to stop eating? Should you make them eat something, anything?
   - What if they have trouble swallowing? What if they choke?

3. Emotional:
   - How long will this dying process take, now you feel ...well... heartless for a selfish thought? It's not heartless, it's normal: almost everyone asks the question at some point, and those who

don't are probably wondering about it quietly and guiltily to themselves.

- Suppose you lose sleep staying at their bedside. How will you manage these emotional ups and down?
- Suppose they die while you are sleeping? Will you feel like you let them down, because they were alone at the moment of death?
- What about your immediate family's needs (if caring for a parent, sibling, or a close friend)? Will you be able to maintain your normal activities with your family during this process? If not, how much will you have to give up and how will it affect your family? And you?
- What if you're afraid to be there when they die?
- What happens if you can't take it anymore?

BREATHE

As you read down this list of potential concerns (we apologize if you didn't think of any of these and you now have a whole new set of worries to deal with!), you may wish for answers to every single one before you go on. Breathe. You don't need to answer all of these questions immediately, or possibly ever. Each walk toward death is individual. Start with the big stuff, the more immediate concerns. Pull out all the official documents; figure out whether there will be a series of doctors' appointments in your immediate future and if so, what the logistics of those appointments might be, and then work forward from there.

You can get the answers to many of the questions above if and when you really need answers. For the physical questions of caregiving, ask nurses and home health care professionals, who are usually forthcoming with practical information. They've seen it before and you won't shock them. Check out financial questions online with AARP or your lawyer if you have one or Legal Aid if you don't and can't afford one.

The answers – if there really are any – to emotional questions are what friends and beer (or wine or long walks or yoga or meditation or prayer or all of the above) are for.

The truth is, there is much in life we really can't control. Instead, we learn to adapt to changing circumstances and needs, (or we fight it hammer and tong, depending on temperament and experience). What matters here is that you get the things in place that you *can* control; try to plan ahead for the potential changes going forward; and remember that, depending on a host of factors in the individual situation, you may never have to deal with even half of this list. Take one step at a time. Don't forget to breathe.

Resources:

National Caregivers Library has many checklists and forms to download

http://www.caregiverslibrary.org/home.aspx

http://www.caregiverslibrary.org/

http://www.caregiverslibrary.org/for-employers.aspxsenior-real-estate.aspx

For Maryland or Massachusetts' MOLST forms visit:

http://marylandmolst.org/

http://molst-ma.org/

Chapter Three

PEOPLE DIE THE WAY THEY LIVE

What would you do if you found out that you only had, say, one year to live? Would you quit your job, take a long vacation, save for your own care or, like one of Sue's patients, who wanted to 'teach her ungrateful son a lesson,' spend as much on the QVC channel as you could from your deathbed? Would you stop burning the candle at both ends? Or run until you crashed and burned? Would you check out of your own life? Or plug in completely, savoring each day with those you loved? Would you get married, divorced, seek love, sever a relationship? Would you dive into religion or seek a spiritual healer? Would you abandon your faith, stay royally pissed off at God, the Universe or whatever name you want to put to your concept of a higher, broader power than our small selves? Or turn to religion for the first time in your life? Would you reconnect with everyone you ever cared about or wronged to say one last word of love, or ask forgiveness? Would you carry on as you had been up until now, feeling that you had lived as good and full and rich a life as possible given your individual circumstances? Would you be grateful for every day that remained? The answer probably depends on who you are.

There are those who, when smacked in the face with the reality that our time here is limited, become great time managers. They realize that life is a precious gift and act accordingly. They cut out everything that no longer has any real meaning in their lives and focus completely on what is most important to them – whether that's spending time with those they love, running around to parties with a bunch of strangers, getting their stamp collection in order, sitting on the sofa smoking and drinking glass after glass of bourbon, or blowing whatever cash they have on the QVC channel. What you would choose might well be very different from what the person, who has been diagnosed as terminal, will focus on. But it's their life, not yours, regardless of how much better you might think you could do it.

The fact that people usually continue to be who they have been all along can be exasperating. It can be tough to deal with – especially if you had hoped that this would be a wake-up call to the person to make the course corrections you think they should be making in the face of this diagnosis. We often know how to lead other people's lives for them better than we know how to lead our own (or at least we think we do). But you can't change people. It's unlikely that the smoker who has been diagnosed with lung cancer will stop smoking unless they simply can't do it anymore (E-cigarettes can be a help, here, though). People won't stop being who they are just because they've been told they have a suddenly limited time horizon. In fact, they may hurry up to get in their last licks. There is in all likelihood very little you as caregiver, loved one, friend can do to change that. Don't make yourself and them crazy trying.

PERSONALITY TIMES TEN

We die the way we live – not our lifestyles or our jobs or the groups we belonged to, but our temperaments, the ways we relate to friends, family, good times and bad – in short, how we as individuals approach life. A diagnosis does not change personality; it dials it up about tenfold. Is your loved one a person who talks about every problem, ache and pain? They will probably talk more now. A partier? You won't be able to catch them at home until they can no longer get out the door, and even then, the party may come to them. Are they private? They will probably close up more or shut down altogether. Some people will be defined by a disease; some will resist, some will carry on gracefully to the end, some will use it to suck all the oxygen out of the room; it depends on who they were before the diagnosis. You know the type:

Stoic
Caregiver: How are you feeling today?
Loved one: Fine!

Denier:
Caregiver: Why did you make that face?
Loved one: I don't know what you are talking about!

Angry:
Caregiver: I am worried. You look like you're in pain.
Loved one: Stop nagging and leave me alone!

Victim:
Caregiver: I am leaving to pick up your prescription and run a few errands.
Loved one: Good for you! At least you're not stuck in the house. Just GO!

Doer:
Caregiver: Let me get your medicine for you
Loved one: Sit down! I'll get it myself

Comedian:
Caregiver: How do you feel?
Loved one: Like a beer. Hang the calories.

Whether they are rational or irrational, lovable or not, controlling or passive, outspoken or reserved, allow them to be the person they are, and figure out how to help them walk that last stretch.

If they are analytical they will want to formulate a plan and stick to it. If they are practical and organized, they will know what they want and do their best to orchestrate it. If they are methodical and considerate, they will try to order their affairs to keep those they leave behind from having to clean up a mess they left and thereby enable loved ones to both grieve and be grateful for the time they shared.

Mary Ann's father had set things in such order that all Mary Ann had to do when he died was make a few phone calls to set in motion what he had put in place. His will already set out an absolutely even split of remaining assets to his four surviving children (Mary Ann's mother always said that they were so careful about being sure they treated each child equally, that they would count out M&M's!). Since Mary Ann was the primary caregiver for both her parents who lived with her and her family for the last three years of their long and happy lives, she had a power of attorney for each parent and was an executor along with one of her two sisters. As a conscientious sister, she had been in regular touch with her far-flung siblings, who also had copies of their parents' wills. Keeping everyone in the loop allowed her siblings to stay connected and staved off what could have been disagreements about decisions leading up to and following the parents' deaths eight days apart in their bedroom in Mary Ann's home. Although her father died at 98 essentially without warning (though with plenty of gradual decline), her 91-year-old mother, who survived him by only eight days, died surrounded by her children and grandchildren. Mary Ann's father, who loved a good party, had even designated money for his wake, at which everyone toasted his long and rich life. Eight days after that wake, the second funeral was held in conjunction with her mother's stated wishes, and family and friends toasted Margaret with Irish Cream over ice. Fitting.

While Mary Ann's parents died of what's termed natural causes – our bodies at some point simply give out like old Chevys – Pat Brack died much younger, leaving just-grown children and a grieving husband behind. She had always been the social director for all her friends, and remained so to the end (and beyond) according to her friend Cheryl Hodgeson.

In a letter to her husband, Pat had written detailed directions for the celebration that she wanted to take place after she died. But, knowing that he would be grief-stricken and possibly distracted, she entrusted the envelope that contained them to a friend. The letter was to be opened by her husband and read in front of two witnesses. The envelope also held money – she didn't want her frugal husband to scrimp on her last hurrah – along with instructions for the party that she wanted him to throw. In addition to the guest list and other details in the letter, she left instructions for her husband that instead of working in the kitchen doing the food and/or acting as bartender himself – jobs that the two of them had always done themselves when having friends in – he was to hire both a caterer and a bartender. For this party, Pat wanted him to be present. She wanted her friends to get drunk and talk about her and have fun, and she wanted her husband in the middle of it all. So they did. It was joyful, uplifting, and for her husband a loving goodbye from his wife.

Sometimes people have an intuitive sense of their impending demise. Like an aura that often precedes a migraine; something feels very different from anything they've felt before. They don't need a clinical explanation; they know what they know based on how they feel. Often they try to tell you, testing your emotional readiness to talk candidly about what they feel with seemingly off-hand remarks: I hope I make it to the wedding day; I hope to see the performance (or as with Sue's father, 'You were right about the diet'). The natural response from the hearer is often an attempt at reassurance: 'Of course you will go to the wedding… the performance,' whatever. But this well-intentioned effort can actually shut the person down if they want to talk about their impending death. Their remark was a gentle test of your willingness to discuss it honestly, and you did not pass (which is one reason so many will tell a hospice worker things they have not told their nearest and dearest). Many don't want to disappoint their loved ones, who may resist these conversations because they believe it is a sign of the person 'giving up.' Yet if there are signals, however subtle – a quick, wistful I'll-never-see-you-again look or a glad-to-have-known-you look directly into your eyes, a word out of the ordinary, a hesitation when they say your name – all of these small things can be potential hints that the person wants to talk.

Unfortunately, many never get a chance at such conversations. Often, the person will talk freely with hired help or paid caregivers in a facility – perhaps they can't bear to see the look of sadness, fear or pity on the faces of those they are soon to leave, or are afraid to initiate a conversation they can't control. If you are lucky, those they've confided in will share the information with you, giving you an opportunity to start a conversation before it's too late. If the person is at home, and you are the caregiver, be alert for signs, or signals that the person wants to talk, either with you or with some other person that they may ask to come see them.

"A dying person seems to want to feel some confidence that you will go on without them," Sue observes. "They want to leave knowing those left behind will be okay, particularly if they are leaving children still at home or a dependent relative. Obviously you are NOT okay with their dying, but eventually after grieving, after time has passed you will be okay and will go on with fond memories of the time you shared with the person."

Sometimes, the person just wants to see someone for the last time, knowing it will in all likelihood be the last time there is any contact with them.

One friend, whose husband lay dying, let his friends know. They came for a last visit, a time, she says, that he and she both treasured. Another friend, whose father lay on his death bed only four months after his wife of 65 years died, flew from New York state to Florida to be with his father one more time. His dad, who had not spoken for two days, greeted him with the only word he could muster; 'Rascal." Affectionate, comradely – the pair had worked together for many years – a lighthearted way to say goodbye.

THE MOM SYNDROME: THAT'S A MEDICAL TERM

Generally, mothers whether 35 or 95, will not die in front of their children. We think it's because most mothers have spent their lives trying to protect their children from pain of one kind or another. They even try to protect their adult children, who may be just as reluctant to let their aged mother go as a child.

"What's most striking to me, is that the children of women in their 90's tend to cling the hardest," Sue says. "It's the seventy-year-old children who can't accept mom not eating, who won't accept her sleeping all the time, whose questions about how to prolong her life seem odd to an onlooker because mom is almost one hundred for Pete's sake! Logic if not experience would tell you she's not going to live forever. But perhaps because they've had Mom for so long, the idea of her leaving is impossible to imagine. Life would seem strange in her absence, the end of an era they never believed would come. Numbers be damned."

"Sometimes you want to tell these children there's a 50-year-old woman in the next room who would love to trade with their mom, that your mom had a good run, heck *you've* outlived the 50-year-old," says Sue. "But as a hospice nurse, I don't say it; I only think it, because I know that a maternal bond can run deep, biologically, emotionally. I know. I'm a mom, too."

Yet even with the Mom Syndrome, people die the way they live. Does Mom regale you (or try to guilt you) with every ache or pain? Then she may die in your presence. Does she share everything? (How would you know? Do you share everything with her?). Or only certain things with you? *You* may want to be with her when 'it' happens, but *she* may not want that. Throughout the many years Sue has been a hospice nurse, she has over and over again watched the inexplicable ability of a mother to wait to die until her children have left the room. This is particularly striking in a person who is in a very deep coma, who does not even react to touch or sound. The minute the children leave the bedside to go to the bathroom or get a drink of water, their mom will take that moment to die. The obvious question is: What part of them is still aware and knows you've left their side? We don't know, but Sue and many other hospice nurses have seen it in action.

Clara had two daughters; Kate lived nearby while Lily lived out of state. Kate left the hospice center to go home and wait for her sister, who was coming from New Jersey. Their mother was unresponsive. Even so, Sue leaned close to Clara and told her that the girls would be back in about an hour and a half.

"Clara did not respond with eye movement or anything to indicate she heard and understood," Sue remembers, "but I told her anyway. Forty-five minutes later I returned to Clara's room to give her an update: The girls should be back in an hour or so."

"I noticed Clara's color was changing," Sue says. "I hoped that she would hang in until they got back so they could be with her when she died."

A half hour later Sue returned again to find Clara guppy-breathing, like a fish out of water.

"Her jaw was moving, but there was not much air passage," Sue says. "I held her hand while Clara took her last breath. Looking back, I got a strange feeling that I walked her to her death."

Fifteen minutes later the daughters returned to the hospice center. As soon as they saw Sue in the hall, they seemed to know their mother was gone and began to cry. Like a mantra Lily kept repeating, "I should have come earlier."

"I asked them: "Did your mom share everything with you?" Sue says now. "I was suggesting that their mom may not have wanted to die in their presence. Kate jumped on the notion immediately. "Lily was her baby," she blurted. "Mom would not die in front of Lily." Lily's tears suddenly stopped, and a flash of understanding crossed her face. I suggested Lily watch for her mom in her dreams, and with animation she recalled a dream she had had of her grandmother after she had died."

WHICH IS HARDER, SLOW OR FAST?

This may not be the way you imagined this relationship would end. In fact, it's clearly not what you want. But consider the alternative: a sudden death – heart attack, accident, war or a crime. A sudden death is full of unanswered questions, disbelief, shock and a lot of mulling over the 'what ifs.'

Slow or anticipated deaths usually mean watching a loved one deteriorate and possibly suffer, which is a difficult journey. But unlike a sudden, unexpected death, it offers the opportunity to get affairs in order and to make this as good a death as it can be. It gives both parties time to right wrongs, to forgive and to make amends. It also allows time for reviewing a life, including acknowledging accomplishments.

One of the men in Sue's care had a conversation with his priest, worried about what was to come because he was not a regular churchgoer. The priest asked how he felt about the children he had raised. The man said he was very proud of his children. "Good fruit does not fall from a bad tree," the priest replied. "This accomplishment is more important [in the scheme of things] than attending weekly services."

Any death presents its own sets of challenges. The shock from a slow death may not be as intense as a sudden death; still, there is an element of surprise when that last breath is taken. Death is death; slow or sudden, we still grieve.

The best we can offer someone with a terminal illness is support of their decisions, a keen ear to pick up even their implied requests for reassurance that their life was worthwhile, an intuitive eye to watch for their vague gestures or expressions of concern or pain that we might be able to alleviate. All of which are opportunities to let them know that they are not alone. This sensitive, conscious connection with another human being can transform a relationship. Giving the dying comfort is not simply kind; it is comforting to you as well. It leaves those remaining with a sense of satisfaction, and the calming knowledge that you did everything you could to ease someone's passage. What matters is not that you did this perfectly — there is no such thing as perfect — it's that you tried.

Chapter Four

SMILE AT ME

For those who are not with the person every day, it can be a shock to see how quickly a human being can change as they are dying. Writer Delia Ephron said that when her sister and fellow writer and collaborator, Nora Ephron began chemo therapy she was regularly mistaken for her twin, yet ten days later, Nora was mistaken for Delia's mother, so dramatic was the physical change.

It's only been a week since you last saw your friend, cousin or colleague. Your recent conversations have been good – reminiscing about old times, talking about books, ballgames, and the balancing acts in life. You've been looking forward to this visit and have put together things that you know he or she would appreciate – several small containers of the person's favorite soup, a couple of books on tape and a recently unearthed picture of the two of you. You come in, pleased to share what you've brought, then stop. The friend you saw last week doesn't look anything like the gaunt person you see now. You freeze knowing that your shock shows on your face, but you can't control it. He looks so different. Like death. Looking at the floor, out the window, anywhere but into his face, you start to say something, but your voice cracks.

You know he's reading your shock in every line of your body. They warned you about how much he had changed – the sunken cheeks, the changed color, the weakness – but the descriptions didn't prepare you for this. You don't know what to do, where to look. What do you do now? Awkward silence. You try to think up something clever. Nothing's coming. Then your friend breaks the ice with a lame joke; he was always better than you in difficult settings. You look him in the eyes and he smiles. A warm glow lights his face. The look is familiar. An old friend has returned. You smile back.

"A smile sent will always return" says an Indian proverb.

A smile can be a magical thing. When you can't find the words, smile. When your loved one looks scary – and you're terrified; it feels like death is all around you – smile at him anyway. A smile is a catalyst for human connection. It says, I'm happy to see you. It says I love you, no matter how you look, no matter how hard this is going to be for either of us.

A smile is not just emotional relief. It's clinically therapeutic. Smiling releases endorphins (neuropeptides), which reduce pain and stress and lift spirits. A smile can boost the immune system, and lower blood pressure. It brightens your face, brightens the face of the receiver and brightens a room. A smile is contagious; pass it along.

A smile makes you feel less stressed out and makes the other person feel wanted and appreciated. You can't change the physical decline you can see, so why make that your focus? You need to look past the exterior to the person you've always known inside. He is not the disease or the condition. He may look different, but he is still the same person in spirit; show him you know that with a smile. Keep it light but keep it real. When there is nothing more to say that he doesn't already know, smile. What matters here is that you are present; you connect.

Some people are afraid a smile sends the wrong message when things are difficult. Especially if the person has been recently diagnosed. If this is the first time you've seen the person, you may feel as though you need to be grim as a sign that you commiserate, that you're mourning with them, for them. Maybe that's what the person wants. But if they don't – and you can take your cue from them – smile. It says you know they are the same person they've always been, that you're glad to see them, and you're prepared to walk beside them, living as much as you can along with them in the time they (and all the rest of us) have left here. Perpetually wearing a grim expression, particularly when you are by your loved one's side, may even make this process harder for them.

One of Sue's colleagues was diagnosed with pancreatic cancer but instead of spending more time at home, she chose to keep coming into work.
"No one at home smiles," she explained. "It's oppressive. Here, people smile at me."

WHAT CAN I SAY?

Talking to a loved one, friend, relative, or colleague who is dying can be frightening. Your heart is breaking; they are leaving you – you don't want them to go, and they most likely don't want to go, either. Panic sets in because this takes you into the unknown, into the face of death. You don't want to face their mortality or what it might mean about your own. You're incredibly uncomfortable, vulnerable. You can't control any of this. Being forced to stand by waiting and watching is agony.

BREATHE

And smile

Don't know what to say? Think: What would I want someone to say to *me?* Would I want them to pretend nothing has changed? Ignore what's coming? Talk about trivialities? Delve into the mystery of life? As with all human relationships, it depends on who the person is, and on your relationship with them.

For clues, think about how they have lived their life up until now. You may have rehearsed what to say on your way, and yet once you get there, worry that nothing you have thought about saying is going to be the right thing. Keep calm and carry on. This is probably not comfortable, but it's also not a performance. You're not on stage. You've come to spend a little time with someone you care about. This may not be comfortable, but knowing that the reason you're there is because you care about them lets you relax a bit so you can get comfortable with being uncomfortable.

What exactly do you say? The best approach is to be honest and speak from the heart. Talk with the person as you always have. Let the conversation unfold and see where it takes you. This is probably hard for them, too.

One popular local radio talk show host, struggling with terminal cancer, finally had no choice but to retire. On his last day on-air, he was being interviewed by another local radio personality who, momentarily forgetting the reason for his colleague's departure said, "That's got to be a great feeling to retire." There was a split-second's pause, when the interviewer realized what he had said. Then the talk show host grunted, "Well, I'd rather not be. As I've often told you: I never wanted to retire!" The interviewer had been trying to make the point that his friend's career had been spent doing what he loved, and he was leaving behind a notable legacy. Unfortunately, the words came out wrong.

Though the men were both pros, usually glib on camera, accustomed to saying all the appropriate things, one had stumbled. There was an awkward pause. We spend so much time pretending that death is not something that happens to us or to those close to us, that we don't know how to respond when we or someone we know is staring it in the face. We don't automatically have a set of 'appropriate' remarks. What we can have, though, is sincerity, and trust in the other person's trust in us. The talk show host simply stated what he felt, corrected the record, and the pair moved on.

Have you suddenly developed foot-in-mouth disease? If you say the wrong thing the person's response will immediately guide you. Apologize and go on. If you totally blow it, apologize all over yourself and get out of the room. You can send a note later, when you've had time to think through what you really want to say. If you don't trust yourself to talk in person, send a note. But even when you say something that you can't believe came out of your mouth you can be forgiven, particularly if you acknowledge it. It's surprising how, when we know that someone cares about us, we can forgive each other.

LAUGH

Laugh? Yes! Some say it's disrespectful to laugh in the face of death, but it's more like defiance, a determination to enjoy every moment in life. If the dying person has a sense of humor, likes to banter, enjoys laughing, joking or clowning around, they probably will still enjoy it all. It's still a part of their personality.

Nancy's father's response to "Nice to see you, Pop," was always, "Nice to be seen!" followed by a big grin. When he lay in bed only days away from dying, she and her brother stood over him. Her brother made a typically black humor joke about the situation and both began to laugh. Her father opened his eyes, looked at both of them, and asked:

"What're you two doing?"

"Having a laugh at your expense, Pop," Nancy replied, patting his arm.

"Oh," he smiled. "Good."

This kind of generosity of spirit takes courage. It takes courage to laugh at your own death, like the young mother Sue knew, who was dying of breast cancer in the early 1980's.

Alice had been diagnosed with terminal cancer. She and her husband planned to visit family a three-hour drive away over the Christmas holidays, but Alice was convinced that she was going to die on the trip. She wondered how that would complicate matters for her family and worried about her husband having to transport her 'dead body across state lines.'

"If it weren't for our seven-year-son," Alice said, chortling, "I'd have him put lots of makeup on me and prop me up in the back seat, so he could get through the tolls, like they did to the aunt in National Lampoon's Vacation."

Alice turned out to be prescient. She died during her visit with her parents, a visit that may well have been a gift to all concerned. But as painful as the loss was for everyone, the memory of Alice's suggestion, and her robust laughter at the picture it conjured in her own mind helped those she left behind.

We are not born with a set of instructions on how to do this thing called dying, so who's making up the rules? Who says laughing is inappropriate, who says it's wrong, who says it's improper? Sadness is one thing, but forced solemnity is another. Just because we laugh, doesn't mean we aren't also grieving. Joni Mitchell's *People's Parties* offers the line: "Laughing and crying: you know it's the same release." Respond from your heart.

We often begin mourning when the diagnosis is made. But mourning doesn't have to be a constant companion. Don't cloud your mind with the disease or the dying process – if that is your only focus you will miss the last opportunities you may have to share the same kind of fun you once had with the person you've known. Laughing can be a way of coping – as can crying – what matters is sharing the time you have together.

We bring our own personalities, knowledge, experience, skills and shortcomings along with us when visiting or caring for the dying. It's difficult to watch someone we love die. It's particularly intense for the family. We can't fix the situation or change the circumstances, but we can help support the person – and help create the best experience we can manage in that last goodbye – by being truly present, active listeners focused on what's being said when someone needs to talk or vent about the situation. And we *can* ask ourselves: 'Am I helping? How can I help?'

THINGS NOT TO SAY

Actual statements made to the dying in hospice care followed with suggestions for more honest alternatives.

1. You'll be up and about soon!	1. How are you feeling?
2. You're doing fine.	2. How is it going?
3. Hey, see you again real soon.	3. I care about you.
4. Hang in there.	4. I'm sorry you're experiencing this
5. Cheer up.	5. I wish you didn't have to go
6. Everything will be all right.	6. Do you want to talk about it?
7. You need to eat something.	7. Can I fix you something to eat?
8. Where's your happy face today?	8. May I just sit with you a while?
9. You can beat this.	9. I really don't know what to say
10. I know how you feel.	10. I'd like to hear how you feel.

Statements like those on the left may spring from a wish to offer encouragement and hope to the person, an attempt to sugarcoat – or deny – the reality of death, but they can also erupt out of anxiety. Dying is an intimate thing. Maybe you are afraid of what the person will tell you, afraid to be that intimately connected to the person and the experience of death. Maybe you're afraid of the demands this will place on you. Or maybe it's the result of your fears about your own death. It's hard to be empathetic when you have not explored your own feelings about death and dying, and most of us have not. (Or if we have, it's usually not gone beyond: "I don't want to do it and I don't want anyone I love to go through it either. End of story.").

Most of us are coming to this situation unprepared, so things sometimes come out wrong. You didn't intend to say 'I know how you feel' since you've obviously not gone through this yourself. Maybe when that last word passes your lips, you think: Yikes! Why did I say that?! (Or maybe the person will retort "Really? You been here before?")

Often we say peculiar things because we aren't present in the moment, we're struggling to read from an unfamiliar script and we feel overwhelmed by what's happening. Instead, we're trying to escape, whether physically or emotionally, or we're running on autopilot, (like the newscaster who congratulated his dying colleague on a retirement that was being forced on him by the progression of a disease). If you fumble, back up and apologize, then keep going. If some of your statements come out backwards, and if you haven't offended the person, laugh at yourself with them; it's just a bump in the road not a major hurdle. Of course, there are some people who can't laugh about it. With them, you have to apologize and then just get the hell out of the room!

For those who have had a terminal diagnosis, but who are not yet in hospice care – and may never be – simply stopping to tell the person the latest office or neighborhood news, read a funny column you knew they'd enjoy, share a book, or watch TV together can be a lift in spirits for both of you. You can acknowledge that you are sorry they are having a tough time without ever alluding to the diagnosis or its likely outcome. Much of human communication and caring is non-verbal.

WHAT THE DYING WANT

- A sense of purpose. Allow them to continue to care for you as well as to participate in their own care if they are able. Don't treat them as an invalid (i.e in-valid). Don't talk about them as if they are not in the room.

- Acceptance of the fact they are dying. The dying person needs to feel free to talk about their feelings and hopes for their family. This is true once *they* have accepted the fact that they are dying. For some, it takes until the last possible moment, for others, it is something they decide early on and wish to acknowledge and deal with. Mary Ann's father, who was a life-loving 98-year-old determined to reach his 100th birthday, (and who had been planning his own centennial party for years), said: "I wouldn't mind dying if it weren't so permanent!"

- To be heard. Do not second-guess their needs and wants. Don't deny the validity of what they say. Learn to be an active listener. Be open to how they feel both physically and emotionally in order to understand their challenges and offer support. Listen to what is NOT being said. You know them. Watch the body language, if they turn their head or avert their eyes when you are speaking, stop. Instead ask a question: Do you want me to leave you for a while? Can I get you anything? Is there anything you want to talk about? And give them time to think before they answer.

- The truth. There is no time for anything else. They see through attempts to 'protect' them from your concerns.

- To be touched: Ask for permission to hold their hand. If they are unresponsive, place your hand *under* theirs.

- Hope. If they slept all day after a surge of pain or because they were exhausted from a slew of visitors, encourage them to listen to their body and sleep. It doesn't necessarily mean the end has come.

- To know how they will die. Most terminal people are not afraid to die; they are concerned with how it will happen, with the moments before death. Like Woody Allen's: "I'm not afraid to die; I just don't want to be there when it happens!"

  Only days before she died, Nancy's mother-in-law, who was tiny and wasted away, but always emphatic, was still sitting at the dining room table when the hospice nurse arrived.

  "Are you in pain?" the nurse asked.

  "No."

  "Are you afraid?"

  "Should I be?" was her immediate and typically defiant response.

- Reassurance that their life had a purpose, a value, and that they made a difference while they were here.

- To unburden themselves

Many dying people will confide in a volunteer, a chaplain, home health aide or nurse rather than the family. When the custodian of this kind of information passes it along to loved ones, the shocked response is often: 'Why are they telling *you* and not their own family (or the people they love most)?'

The answer is simple. No pressure. Just as some people can confide in strangers at the airport or in a café, knowing there will be no repercussions at home, the dying can confide in a volunteer, hospice worker or aid simply because no matter what long-buried secrets or hopes, what shattered dreams or disappointments they confide, they know it will not affect the hospice worker the way they perceive the information might hurt, anger or disillusion their loved ones. The professional has no personal or emotional baggage concerning this person's death, so they will simply listen as one human being to another without offering solutions or recriminations. Regardless what confidence the dying person offers to the paid caregiver or other professional, it will not change the relationship.

Even when the dying person tries to initiate these kinds of conversations, family members or loved ones may not be willing to listen. Whether it's because they are afraid of what they might be told, or are pretending (hoping) that the dying person will somehow rally hardly matters. The dying person may hope for a rally too, but is usually willing to face the reality of the situation. Their offering to have a genuine human-to-human conversation about their most deeply held convictions, regrets, secrets or hopes is (usually) a gift that they hope the loved one will accept. What matters here is how open you are, and whether or not this conversation will ease the dying loved one.

Sometimes the dying worry about:

- The stress on the family
- Finances and how much will be left after they are gone
- Saying goodbye
- Making amends
- The meaning of life
- If they will be alone at that last moment. (Arrangements can be made to insure someone is with them – conscious or not – if that is their wish/concern).

Below is a list of twelve questions hospice workers often ask the dying, who are, after all, leaving everything they've known here behind. But remember that not everyone wants to talk. Don't force it.

TO EASE OPEN DIALOGUE:

1. Is there anything we can do to make this easier for you?
2. Is there someone you would like to talk to [before you die]?
3. What are you afraid of? Of dying? Of pain? Of leaving?
4. Do you have any regrets?
5. Is there something that you still want to do that you have not been able to do?
6. Do you worry about someone you are leaving behind?
7. Would you like someone to know something that you have not been able to put into words before now?
8. Are you spiritually at peace - do you need help to prepare?
9. What do you believe is beyond this life?
10. Are you excited or fearful about what is to come?
11. What areas of your life have given you the most security or comfort or pleasure and how can you use this to help you move on?
12. Do you want many visitors or just close family?

If you just broke out in hives reading these questions, it's okay. A good way to help a person talk is to ask about prized possessions, collections or hobbies. Sharing a quick story will help open the door to conversation, but do not go into elaborate descriptions of your own experiences; remember this exercise is to get the dying talking, not you. Ask them to tell stories. Big talk usually starts with small talk.

If the person has always been reserved there may not be any deathbed confessions or effusive statements of how much those they leave behind have meant to them. Men often will be reluctant to say the words 'I love you' to sons in particular, saying that it's unnecessary, that 'they know how I feel.' Although those the dying leave behind may trust in the person's love for them, hearing it said aloud can be a parting gift. However, there can be other ways to convey it without saying the words.

Several days before he died, Nancy's father didn't know either her or her stepmother. Lying in bed, a look of bewilderment on his face, he stared at the two of them as each leaned over to give him a kiss.

"Do you know who this is?" Nancy's brother asked their father, bringing his stepmother close to his father's face.

"No."

"Do you know who this is?" he asked, doing the same thing with Nancy.

"No."

"Do you know who I am?" he asked.

"You're my son, Chris!" he said emphatically, an affirmation of how much Chris meant to him, regardless of his reluctance to articulate it throughout their lives, and a last gift to his only son.

What matters is that we recognize when a dying loved one is giving someone a gift like this and accept it with gratitude.

Chapter Five

CAREGIVER 101:

Whether you are going to be the primary caregiver, part-time or helping caregiver or are a relative or friend, who is setting things up for a hired primary caregiver, there's a list of the things that may and/or definitely will be needed to have on hand. These lists are online as well; you can download them from our website to use them as checklists.

Some people are able to care for themselves physically for the most part until the very end. Others need help from time to time. Still others need ongoing assistance. Each situation is unique to the person or people involved and their circumstances. But there are some general rules of thumb and tips that may help the caregiver, depending on what exactly the caregiver is being called on to do.

Before we go farther, let us give you a little encouragement. If you're thinking OMG! I can't do this! Let me out! Let me out! Take a deep breath and wait for a minute to calm yourself. For most people, this will not come easily, at least at first. It will take some adapting to. But take heart in the fact that human beings can adapt, amazingly and gracefully, to a wide range of situations. Whatever we do repetitively usually becomes routine.

In an odd echo of Driving Miss Daisy, *the hired live-in caregiver that Nancy's mother-in-law had for many years was not formally trained for the job. She had begun her employment as the cleaning person. But over time, as her employer's ability to do things for herself declined, Josephine was asked to move into the house. Soon, she became the full time weekday caregiver, and her duties grew to include more and more personal care. Josephine may not have sought it, but she grew accustomed to doing the bodily things over time, and in fact, despite the difficulties, grew to love her employer. Her employer loved her in return.*

STOCKING THE SICKROOM

1. At least 4 extra pillows or a wedge pillow for support of a bedbound person.
2. A box of bendable straws.
3. A rubber sheet to protect the mattress, (or a plastic leaf bag across the middle of the bed).
4. A box of disposable gloves
5. Disposable pads, briefs or undergarments. If the person is overweight and too heavy to move frequently to change a diaper use

the pads and pull up a part between the thighs to collect any discharge.
6. A urinal and bedpan. Buy or rent a commode. Mix a small amount of household cleaner with water in a spray bottle for easy cleaning of the commode. Use it each time to clean out the urinal and bedpan.
7. Make a solution of bleach and water to keep at hand in a spray bottle for quick clean ups.
8. Barrier cream to protect the person's skin. Avoid heavy paste-like creams; trying to remove them during cleanups can damage the skin. Instead, try moisture barrier creams (available from most drugstores and pharmacies) enriched with vitamins A and D, and mix the cream with cornstarch to serve as a protection against wetness.

SAFETY FIRST FOR YOU AND THE PERSON

1. Remove any scattered rugs and clutter that you could easily trip over, especially when tired or hurried. Don't forget the extension cords, computer cords and plugs, and cell phone chargers.
2. USE and then DISPOSE of disposable gloves after each use.
3. Wash your hands with soap and water every time you come in contact with your loved one to prevent the spread of a possible infection to either of you.
4. Always clean the skin after an episode of incontinence then apply a barrier cream to protect skin. Mix the cream with cornstarch to serve as a barrier to wetness.
5. Make up the bed with a PULL SHEET that you will use to help reposition a person unable to move him or her self. To make a pull sheet, take a flat bed sheet, fold it in half crosswise and place over the plastic bag or rubber sheet. This will keep the plastic from direct contact with the person. The pull sheet can be used to pull a person up in bed by securing the sheet in each hand to slide the person in bed. You may need two people for this procedure depending on the person's size, weight and ability to help. Your ability to do this will also depend on the position of the bed. It may help to shift the bed so you can get behind the headboard, as Nancy did with her father's hospital bed. His bones were so fragile from cancer that pulling him up under his arms was not possible without causing a fracture, so Nancy got behind the head of his hospital bed and gently worked her arms beneath his back on either side of his spine. Once she had his shoulders at the inside of her elbows, she could slowly move him up into a better position.
6. Always tell the person what you intend to do before taking action; speak in a tone they can hear, touch their hand or arm while addressing them. Make eye contact so they don't startle or fight you.

7. In shifting or repositioning a person, keep their body close to you: avoid reaching, which can strain your back or shoulder muscles or cause a fall for both of you.

USE GOOD BODY MECHANICS

Bend at the knees not the waist.
Keep feet about shoulder width apart.
Keep back straight.
Lift with your legs.

1. Again, tell the person your intention before you act; many people have a fear of falling when they are not able to move themselves.
2. Then, remove all pillows.
3. Place their arms across the abdomen or tell them to 'give yourself a hug' if they are able. Straighten the legs and position them close together.
4. Using a pull sheet, slide the person toward you, bend their top knee and direct it to the opposite side of the bed. Lift the pull sheet, lifting the person's back off the bed and tuck 1-2 pillows under the back. This will relieve the spine from direct contact with the bed.
5. Place a pillow between the knees, and a pillow under the top arm for support.
6. An easy way to pull someone up in bed: get behind the head board if possible, have the person bend their knees and push with their feet while you pull under their armpits to slide them up. If the person can no longer assist, you should not try this; it could be too much strain on your back and injure you.

BATHING:

1. Bathing is not a daily requirement, especially if bathing is difficult. Wash face, hands and genital area daily. Bathing stimulates circulation and provides movement of the extremities. It also presents an occasion to check the skin for any redness that could be a sign of pressure sores.
2. Use less soap and water than you would in a bath or shower; it will be easier to remove and less drying to the skin.
3. Apply lotion to back and buttocks to stimulate circulation.
4. Use an electric toothbrush. If the person has stopped eating, buy oral swabs to clean the mouth and gums. Prop their head up with pillows to prevent choking during this procedure.

5. Shave with an electric razor only – particularly if there is weight loss and the cheeks are sunken.

6. If dressing is difficult, cut clothing straight up the back so shirts, blouses etc. can be tucked under the sides after arms are placed into the sleeves.

7. Keep hair short, check with local barbers/hair dressers to find someone who will come to your home.

Listening to books on tape while doing chores and providing care – especially during bathing and feeding, which both take time, can help both you and the person. Find a book you both enjoy or music.

On the old TV show, MASH, one episode, which purported to be a series of one-on-one interviews with the doctors and nurses in the MASH unit, had Margaret Hoolihan, the head nurse, explaining how a young female nurse could bathe a young solider with a minimum of embarrassment or discomfort to both.
She said that when you bath a person, look them in the eyes and try to keep up conversation about something unrelated as you gently soap and then rinse, and pretty soon, it's done.

TIP for Giving Regular Medication:

This is often a worry to caregivers. Did I give the prescribed medication? This morning? Or was it yesterday? Don't fret! A simple way to know for sure is to set up a cheap, schedule-marked med-dispenser made from an empty egg carton. Label the lid with the times the medicine is to be given. Each evening, fill the sections with all medicine needed for the next day. If the morning medicine is still in its section by 2p.m., you actually did forget. It's probably best to skip the dose to prevent overdosing the person, but consult the physician for the specific circumstances.

WHEN GIVING MEDICATION

1. Elevate the person's head before administering medicine to prevent choking.

2. Do not crush any medicine unless you check with the pharmacist. Some have protective coatings, which are there either to prevent irritation to the stomach lining or to prevent stomach acid from diminishing the effects of the drug. Crushing others could release all the medicine at once and cause problems. If medicines *can* be crushed, you can try dissolving them in a very small amount of hot water, and allowing the mix to cool before giving it.

3. Adding a few drops of juice helps to mask the taste. (Again, check with the pharmacist to be sure which juices will not adversely affect the medication.).

4. If the person can swallow soft foods easily, try floating the pills on applesauce, pudding or ice cream. Keep the amounts of food small; when appetite is fair to poor, you want to make sure they get all the prescribed medicine and not just a portion.

5. If the person can't swallow at all and they need the medication, you can insert the medication rectally with the aid of a lubricant such as butter or Crisco, which will be absorbed. Do not use petroleum jelly.

TIP: Be sure, when anything is given by mouth, that the head is elevated to prevent choking.

CHANGE OF WATCH TIP: If several friends/family will be sharing in the role of caregiver, doing shifts or doing a day or days at a time, establish a caregiver log. The log should be kept in one place – the kitchen is often a good central location. Each caregiver needs to write the date and times of service as a way to communicate what has or has not taken place. It's also a place to record questions regarding care to be sure they get answered.

The caregiver will list food/drink intake, bathroom breaks or note if the person has not gone during their stay (since it may be an issue that needs to be addressed). Also note any activity, i.e. 'walked around the house,' 'stayed in bed.' List of all medicines given, *especially* any pain medicine given; note the dose, how many times it was given and at what times. Also note whether it was effective. Note any new complaints – nausea, vomiting, constipation – and what action was taken for example: called the doctor, new prescription is to be delivered.

You may wonder why, if you will see your replacement and give that person a verbal report, you should bother with all this documenting. Because, documenting not only helps to jog memory (did he/she say they gave one dose at 2p.m. or two doses at 1 p.m.?), it offers a steady record for anyone else who needs to take over for even a short period of time. It offers guidance and confidence to caregivers, especially those for whom this is a new or very short-term role. If you need to find someone to act as a fill-in for a day or two, they can read back and see what has been done. It's not rocket science; it's just common sense communication for all involved.

Don't forget that a little word of encouragement for your replacement goes a long way.

BEDSORES

When a person stops eating and drinking and is bedbound, even the best of care cannot always prevent a bedsore. Good skin depends on a healthy, hydrated body. If a reddened area forms, try to keep direct pressure off the spot. Massage the area gently with lotion, which also stimulates circulation to the area. If a break in the skin develops, clean the area and apply an over-the-counter antibiotic cream and a bandage.

DON'T beat yourself up if a bedsore develops. The person's body is no longer replenishing lost cells. Sometimes even the best cared for person can develop a bedsore when the skin is like gossamer. IT'S NOT YOUR FAULT.

FOR SOMEONE WHO IS VERY CLOSE TO LEAVING:

Place a pillow under each flank, place a pillow under the knees and another one under the lower legs, leaving the heels suspended over the edge of the pillow. If the person is in a hospital bed, elevate the head of the bed 45 degrees.

If the person has audible congestion, raise the head of the bed 60 degrees. In a regular bed, elevate the head with two pillows. The pillows you have already placed under each flank open up the front of the chest, allowing for easier breathing. Elevating the head of the bed facilitates gravity by keeping any secretions from collecting in the back of the throat. The pillows under the flank also keep the spine floating without direct pressure. The pillows under the legs alleviate discomfort in the lower back.

The fear of being with a dying person at the moment of death is shared by many, regardless of age. Nancy's mother-in-law's caregiver, was afraid to be there at the moment of death—and expressed her concern. But, because she had developed a strong bond over the years with her employer, and because she had grown gradually accustomed to dealing with her employer's bodily needs, and because the family offered her steady encouragement, she was not only able to see it through to the end, she was with her employer at the moment of death. In fact, she sat with the body for an hour, saying goodbye to both the relationship with her employer and to this time in her own life, before calling the family.

"I promised her I would do it," she said, "and I was afraid, but I did it, and I'm glad I did it!"

Resources

Cancer Resource Center

(415) 885-3693.

Compassionate Care of the Terminally Ill

http://www.ncbi.nlm.nih.gov/pmc/articles/PMC406380/

Diabetes Association health care resources

http://diabetes.healthcareresourcesonline.org/

Caring for a Terminally Ill Child: A Guide for Parents

http://www.cancer.net/coping/end-life-care/caring-terminally-ill-child-guide-parents

Chapter Six

CARING FOR THE CAREGIVER

Rarely is anyone focused on the caregiver, which makes you feel guilty for even bringing yourself into the equation; it's all about the person who's leaving, isn't it? Well, yes and no. Yes, because of course you want to offer the best care to the person whose time here is winding down. BUT – and it's a biggie – no, in that caregiving, especially if it's a job for which you've not been formally trained (and few of us have) is not only a huge learning curve, which makes it tiring intellectually, it's demanding emotionally and physically, too.

Caregiving for a terminally ill person is a role that usually has been thrust upon you with little or no time to prepare, and it can leave you feeling stuck, resentful, and wanting to bolt – normal responses that serve up guilt on a platter. Or maybe you feel guilty that you, in all likelihood, will survive the other person, or feel guilty being worried about the impact that the loss of them will have on you. (Guilt has so many wonderful triggers).

To assuage the guilt – an unnecessary burden added to an already challenging time – you might be tempted to martyr yourself, mashing down your own needs to focus totally on the other person. You may even get accolades and reinforcement for doing that. But unless there is *absolutely* no other option (and there usually is) martyrdom is not your best choice.

BREATHE, and think for a moment.

To be an effective caregiver, you need to take care of yourself, even though sometimes that may feel selfish. It's not. It's practical. If you don't take care of yourself, you could end up needing care, too.

If you're intellectually on board with taking care of yourself, but are still struggling with residual guilt, consult sensible friends and/or trusted confidents to help assuage – or at least help you calibrate – the guilt. Contact a support group. People who are going through the same things you are will immediately recognize where you are emotionally, and their urging you to look after yourself may not only help you, but them, too.

Still can't shuck it? Then stuff the guilt for considering your own needs into a psychological closet for the moment, because there are practical things you need to deal with before you try to unpack and sort through that particular emotional suitcase.

TAKING CARE OF YOUR BODY

The absolute bottom-line basics for your body are food, water and rest.

FOOD: You need to eat – and this doesn't mean candy bars and big-bucket chicken with a side of fries. Your immune system needs support, so be sure you're getting real meals. Roast a chicken; it takes 10 minutes to stuff a bird into the oven in a roasting pan with a few onions and carrots. There's a great meal right there. Then, later, when you've had a rest or maybe the next morning, take what's left of the meat off the bones, and save it for chicken salad or noodle casserole or curried chicken with veggies. Meanwhile, use the bones, bits of meat, pan juices, skin, everything to make stock, which with very little additional time and effort will then become a vat of homemade soup. (Chicken soup is also clinically therapeutic). You can put some in the freezer that you can take out and stick in the microwave whenever you need something to eat. Keep containers of roasted vegetables, lettuce and some cheese in the fridge, ingredients for quickly assembled substantial salads or wraps. Make a frittata, (basically a baked omelet), which takes about 10 minutes of prep time. Keep fresh fruit on hand for snacks. (See Food for Thought: recipes and ideas).

Each of these things takes a small investment in time and energy, but pays off big in several ways: these suggestions are easy to do since they can be done in snatches; and the resulting nourishment and taste satisfaction can have a huge impact in helping you maintain your health. And they're economical since they don't rely on industrially prepared food. A roasted chicken, or pot roast, salad and soup will sustain you for nearly a week and support your immune system unlike fatty, sugary preservative-laden stuff (which you may crave, but that not only doesn't help you, it ultimately taxes your body). This doesn't mean you don't get to treat yourself to a Snickers bar or ice cream on bad days, but it's important not to use the excuse of being tired and overwhelmed to live on them.

WATER: Stay hydrated. We often forget to do this – especially when we're immersed in something – yet it's of key importance to our health. Aging patients can even show signs of dementia simply through dehydration, a fact that should tell all of us how critical staying hydrated really is. (This is a different issue from whether or not to push fluids into a person who is perhaps retaining fluid and is close to death). We can also mistake a need for water or some kind of hydrating liquid – tea, juice, beer (the existence of which Ben Franklin declared to be a sign that God loves us and wants us to be happy) – for hunger. Start off, always, with a glass of water or tea or something liquid before eating. Have a glass that you sip at while preparing a meal or doing some other stationary chore.

REST: You need decent sleep. It can be challenging, depending on the circumstances and the person you're dealing with. Take a power nap in the afternoon if you need to and are able to manage it, or turn down an invitation you don't really want to accept anyway so you can crash on the sofa. (But don't turn down every invitation, thinking you shouldn't go out and have fun. Fun can be incredibly restorative and healthy.).

This may all sound pretty basic – and it is, actually – but it gets shoved aside, often for days or weeks, while you're busy. You may not wake up to what you should have been doing to keep yourself going until you start to come down with the worst case of bronchitis you've ever had or even, as one friend of Sue's did, walking pneumonia.

TAKING CARE OF YOUR SPIRIT

EXERCISE:

The endorphins produced while exercising have been proven to lower stress hormones, (which tend to add belly fat), increase serotonin, (which elevates mood), and increase dopamine, (which helps with sleep).

- Try yoga. Get some basic or beginner DVD's if yoga is new to you. It helps stretch tired and stiff muscles, reduces stress, and helps maintain good balance.
- Walk – at any pace that's comfortable. Walking gets you out of the house and breathing fresh air (well, presumably fresh air – out of the house is a good thing even if the air quality isn't pristine). It provides a change of scenery, helps to clear your head and stimulates your senses with colors, textures and scents.
- Incorporate walking into your errands. Park at the end of the parking lot and walk. Take the stairs instead of an escalator. Moving keeps your joints lubricated and can help thwart aches and pains.
- Run or jog, which produces endorphins

KEEP UP YOUR SOCIAL LIFE

Say yes to an invitation – or issue one for lunch or coffee with a friend – and go! You do not have to be perpetually at the side of your love one.

They may even feel guilty for putting you in the caregiver's role, and want you to have a respite.

Can't get out? Call a friend on the phone for some conversation. Connection, laughter, commiseration, venting with trusted people can relieve some of the stress and do wonders for your outlook.

Avoid difficult people, even if they are friends or family. They drain your energies unnecessarily.

KEEP A JOURNAL

Have fun with it, use pictures and/or words from that stack of magazines you've been meaning to get to. Congratulate yourself for coping through a day without incident, note something wonderful, or just vent. Purging on paper can help get things off your chest and offers a surprising amount of relief. If it's not something you want to reflect on (or have anyone else read), burn it. Sue's friend kept a journal while going through a divorce (another wrenching loss). The day the divorce was final, her friend poured a glass of wine, started a fire in the fireplace and burned the journal, a very cathartic experience that left her feeling free. On the other hand, Mary Ann didn't keep a journal while she was walking her parents through their last months and days, and now wishes she had that diary as a way to look back on what was a difficult but ultimately satisfying and sometimes funny time in their lives.

Allen Polansky, whose wife, Barbara, was diagnosed with cancer in late February 2000, says journaling helped him enormously while he was going through the months leading to Barbara's death.

"We were running from doctor to doctor," he remembers, "and she turned to me one day and said, 'How are you doing?' I said, 'I'm fine.' And she paused, knowing me much better than I knew myself and she said, 'You're not. You should see somebody.' After a little soul searching, (it took five minutes — I hope it doesn't say anything about the size of my soul!) I decided to take her advice. After a few sessions, [the therapist] suggested journaling."

Polansky agreed, but had no idea how to do it.

"My first thoughts were to write down raw emotions and label them, like I was starting a filing system" he says. "But after a while, I found there could be a lot of release in private — you could say things in your notebook that you couldn't say to people. You could get out the kind of emotions that most people couldn't accept without some professional training. It didn't solve anything, but it did get it out, and it helped."

As fulltime caregiver, there will probably be times you'll snap at the person. It's normal — you're tired, angry at the situation, possibly scared and frustrated. Don't beat yourself up over it. If it's a one-time occurrence, let it go. If it becomes a pattern, beat the pillows, have a cry, either alone or with a friend, get some help.

And don't be afraid to ask your doctor for some chemical help for depression (especially if you're on the verge of diving into a bottle of booze or something you found in the medicine cabinet that should be taken only under a doctor's care). A little prescribed medication under a physician's supervision is a temporary solution to a finite situation, but it could make the difference between your feeling as though you can cope and sitting in a corner whimpering. It doesn't define you as a failure or an incompetent caregiver; it says that you recognize that you would function better – and more happily for both you and your loved one – with a little help.

CAREGIVER TIP: Exercise for the lungs. It's surprising but we're often unaware we're half-holding our breaths, breathing shallowly, which is not good for our stress levels. To reduce stress and increase lung capacity, try to make the opportunity to do the following exercise each day while caring for a dying loved one.

1. Inhale through the nose, hold for a count of four.
2. Slowly, exhale through the mouth for a count of eight.
3. Repeat several times before you resume normal breathing.

ENLISTING HELP WITHOUT GUILT

Call on people. We know we've said this earlier, but it's a reminder – in case you're reading this sequentially, or a head's up in case you're skipping around. Get in touch with friends, co-workers, members of the person's (and your own) religious organization, clubs, neighborhood, community or network. The more people you have available to help, the less stress you will feel. Do you know someone working in health care? They may be a great resource for finding equipment, daily care or respite care. They may also know – or help to chase down – how to get things covered through insurance. The primary care doctor and/or his office staff can also be good resources for this kind of info. Helpful organizations are listed at the end of this chapter.

If you are alone and the family is scattered across the country or internationally, you as fulltime caregiver may need to hire periodic assistance to give you a much-needed break. Does the person need round the clock care? If so, perhaps hire someone during the night so you can get critical sleep or during the day so you can continue to work. Even if a single person can't sign up for regular duty, most people will agree to do at least one night, or one day now and again, which can be a salvation. Some may offer to drive the person to and from regular doctors' or hospital visits, get groceries or pick up dry cleaning, whatever. Take them up on it. People want to help. It's good karma, and we all know we might need a helping hand down the road.

If someone says they would love to help but are too far away, ask for regular contact – cards, letters, emails, flowers – any little thing to let the person and you know you are not alone. Sometimes, creative friends will step into that role with amazing generosity.

Pat Brack had a secret Santa when Pat was in the hospital. The secret Santa began by leaving a partridge in a pear tree ornament at the foot of her hospital bed and continued through the twelve days of Christmas leaving little things – two red candles, three sprigs of holly, and so on – then kept going for months afterward with little things left in Pat's mailbox. It was an enormous morale booster for Pat, who never did learn the identity of her secret Santa. (It was Cheryl Hodgeson, a nurse friend, who went to great lengths to keep from being discovered).

"I just want [whoever it was] to know what a difference it made looking forward to their visits and knowing that someone cared that much," Pat wrote.

If they offer to contribute to the caregiver's relief fund, which will be used to hire respite care so you can take a break, don't be too proud to accept. Helping to pay for in-home respite care will go a long way to assuaging their guilt for not being there (sometimes guilt can be helpful), and it will go a long way toward keeping you from burning out or getting sick.

Don't overlook nieces, nephews, and grandchildren in this wide-net recruitment, even for a single or very short-term specific thing, like an errand that you simply can't manage at the time it needs to be done. Keeping a list of potential helpers with their contact info by the phone will help.

TIP: A website or Facebook page, which is something the younger generation can do to help, can make things easier to coordinate, especially for last-minute changes and needs. A Facebook page helps to keep people connected and gives the children a proactive role in the process. It also cuts down on having to have the same conversations over and over on the phone every day, which can be very wearing to say nothing of time-consuming. Additionally, it's a place where people can sign up for specific jobs, even at nearly a moment's notice – bringing food, doing errands, grocery shopping, etc. – which can relieve the caregiver of the job of coordinator. It's also an easy place to give updates and let folks know what you need.

The more a caregiver can do to seek out and foster support from others during this time, the less stressful and more sustaining the whole experience will be. This is all part of life.

One of our friends, who owned and ran a two-person business with her husband, Bill, spent the last year of her life going through a rigid and demanding series of chemo treatments for metastasized breast cancer. The treatments were given three times a week at a hospital an hour's drive away from their home and business. To enable Bill to keep the business going and pay the bills, a friend orchestrated a team of volunteers to take Beth to and from her treatments. Neighbors, friends, and others signed up to drive – some only once, some for a regular day each week for several weeks at a time. One volunteer, a retired businessman, who had met the couple only once, and who had never done anything like this before, signed up for a weekly run that he performed for several months. He later said that the conversations, which ran the gamut from spiritual to meditative to hilarious, that he had with Beth on those drives were experiences he would treasure for the rest of his life.

CAREGIVER TIP: Ask for help when you need it.

We know that asking for help can be difficult. Even anguishing.

"We've never been apart in 44 years," Debbie said crying over the phone to the nurse at the hospice center.

Her days were consumed by Bob's needs. Bob had ALS aka Lou Gehrig's disease, an eventually terminal condition that affects different people in different ways. Some are unable to speak and swallow; others might have use of their arms but not their legs. Still others lose function on only one side of the body, like a stroke. In Bob's case, it robbed him of the use of all extremities, making him totally dependent. Once the strong family breadwinner, he was unable to move anything but his head. His wife, Debbie, was his sole caregiver. Each morning, the first thing she did was strap him into a hydraulic lift and move him from his chair to a portable potty. This procedure took anywhere from 30-45 minutes. She then cleaned him while he was still suspended in the lift, and completed his bath when he returned to his recliner. Breakfast, another time-consuming task, occasionally stimulated another lift to the potty.

This was the start of Debbie's day, every day, seven days a week, 365 days a year. Yet she not only did not ask for help, but resisted accepting any from hospice or any other potential source of respite care.

Hospice staffers understand that some find it almost impossible to let go of the caregiver's role, even for a short period. The reasons are varied – uncertainty about the care their loved one will receive, guilt at turning the job over to someone else, even possessiveness. But whatever the reasons, it is important for caregivers to take time to restore themselves. Some are unaware how debilitating caregiving can be. Debbie hardly had time to shower or eat; all her energies were directed toward Bob's care.

It took many conversations, including repeated urgings from Bob, to convince Debbie to take a much-needed break. Finally she agreed to admit him to the hospice center for five days. Unfortunately, she couldn't let go. She had trouble sleeping and called the center several times each day, crying and berating herself for leaving him, seeking validation for the decision. The hospice staff urged her to 'have some fun, read a book, visit your grandchildren.' She spent time cooking for her daughters, food shopping, and running errands, but did not take any desperately needed down time for herself. Routines, even such challenging, demanding routines, can be incredibly tough to let go of. It often takes time to readjust — 'several days to turn around on the carpet' is the way one friend put it, while watching her dog circle a rug preparing to lie down. Hospice staff encouraged Debbie to send Bob to the center once a month to refresh her soul — especially important where the need for care can be long term. Respite care can become the new, acceptable, even welcome, routine. The hardest thing can be taking that first step.

HOW TO KNOW YOU NEED MORE HELP:

You're forgetting things you normally recall easily.
You're tired all the time, even after a good night's sleep.
You hardly stop to eat.
You're more irritable than usual.
You're perpetually on the verge of tears.
You feel trapped.
Your friends keep telling you to take a break. (This is a big heads-up).

WHAT TO DO:

Jettison some of your other commitments if they have become a chore — committee meetings, volunteering to bring cupcakes for a class trip, driving Aunt Zuzu to bridge every week. You have enough on your plate. Those things (or others) will still be available to jump back into later if you choose.

Take a break for a day — go to a movie, go shopping for yourself, go to a sports event, a play, a concert or go sit on the beach, a hilltop, in a meadow. Don't forget to breathe deeply while you are doing that. Weed the garden if it helps return you to the simple pleasures of life. Nancy spent portions of her father's last illness weeding and picking the beans in her vegetable garden, an exercise that was both contemplative and productive. It was also a visible reminder that there is a natural cycle to life and death is a part of it.

Take a break for a weekend. Many nursing homes provide respite care for this kind of caregiver-restoring need. Do it even if you feel guilty about it.

Get a massage. A massage is not only relaxing but it also drains the body's lymphatic system of built-up toxins.

Don't give up a hobby, sport, craft, chess in the park, committee meetings, choir – whatever engages your mind and spirit – if you don't want to and can still fit them in. These things can nourish the soul, help restore your energies and keep you connected to a wider community in ways that can help carry you forward when your loved one is gone.

Let some things go. In caregiving, you've taken on what can be a full time job. Keep that in mind. The house doesn't need to be immaculate, the dishes done the minute a meal is over, the laundry folded and stowed as soon as the dryer is finished. Relax your standards a little. (Anyone who criticizes or makes remarks about how clean and organized you used to be automatically gets saddled with a job improving whatever they've criticized!)

Get some professional help. Carla sought out a therapist, who assessed the situation and periodically gave Carla simple, straightforward tasks to accomplish such: as take a walk every day for 2 weeks, Then: spend a half hour every day reading a book you've always wanted to read. Each task brought Carla back into her own, individual life and helped to calm her.

Laugh at the bizarre and absurd. It helps.

Stay present in the moment. Clean the slate every day i.e. try not to carry around the burdens of yesterday and the day before, bearing in mind that this too shall pass.

Forgive yourself for not being perfect at this. Things will blindside you. A terminal patient can be coasting along for weeks then a new symptom pops up with the sunrise. Now what? Call the doctor? Make another trip to the emergency room? You manage to get this symptom quelled. A week goes by, another symptom, another problem. Forgiving yourself for not being perfect at this (especially if you are a Type A personality accustomed to being good at everything you do) will help as things change and you need to adapt to a new normal.

RESOURCES

Caring for the Caregiver – Hope and Help for the Caregiver
Caring Circle meetings are support groups run by a trained moderator.
Phone: 516-921-0755
http://caringforthecaregiver.org/

HelpGuide.org offers advice and resources for caregivers.
http://www.helpguide.org/elder/caring_for_caregivers.htm
http://www.helpguide.org/elder/respite_care.htm
National Cancer Institute
http://www.cancer.gov/cancertopics/coping/caring-for-the-caregiver/page1
Live Help online chat:
https://livehelp.cancer.gov/app/chat/chat_launch
http://www.cancer.org/Treatment/index

Phone
1-800-4-CANCER

Cancer Resource Center
(415) 885-3693.

World Federation for Mental Health's Caring for the Caregiver: Why Your Mental Health Matters When You Are Caring for Others.
http://www.wfmh.org/PDF/Caring%20for%20the%20Caregiver%2011_04_09%20FINAL%20(3).pdf

Family Caregiving Alliance
http://www.caregiver.org/caregiver/jsp/content_node.jsp?nodeid=847

Family Caregiver AllianceNational Center on Caregiving

785 Market Street, Suite 750

San Francisco, CA 94103
(415) 434-3388
(800) 445-8106

Area Agency on Aging
For caregiver support groups, respite providers, and other caregiving services. Eldercare Locator:(800) 677-1116www.eldercare.gov

Interim HealthCare National Headquarters
1601 Sawgrass Corporate Parkway

Sunrise, FL 33323
(800) 338-7786
http://www.interimhealthcare.com/

Diabetes Association health care resources
http://diabetes.healthcareresourcesonline.org/
Compassion and support for end of life scenarios:
http://www.compassionandsupport.org/
http://www.compassionandsupport.org/index.php/resource_directory/co
mprehensive_resources_and_related_topics
Respite care to relieve caregivers:
http://www.helpguide.org/elder/respite_care.htm

Caregivers: 10 tips for caregivers at bottom of page
http://www.helpguide.org/elder/caring_for_caregivers.htm

Chapter Seven

FOOD AND THE CASSEROLE BRIGADE

The first thing some of us think about when we want to support someone with a serious illness is providing food. Depending on the person's condition and disease – as well as your culinary bent – food may be a help or a burden to the person and their caregiver. There is a growing contingent of people who believe many diseases, cancer and diabetes foremost among them, are preventable or even curable with diet; certainly, we've seen the societal damage poor eating has produced. While good nourishment of all kinds is a key component in health, food is also probably not going to stop a terminal disease or condition from taking its ultimate course. Having said that, there *are* things conscientious cooks can do to help.

There are strategies for coping with difficulties in eating, particularly while patients are undergoing treatments of various kinds. Oddly, many physicians are silent on the subject, as though food is too touchy-feely to be professional and scientific. (Or maybe is not in their purview, or is too intrusive or won't make any kind of difference in the experience of the patient.). Luckily, there is a growing recognition among mainstream medical practitioners that nutrition – i.e. truly good food – needs to be part of the equation.

Being given ready-made good meals can be a huge help to someone who has his or her hands full with caregiving. To be a truly supportive part of the support team, you can offer – gently, without insistence – healthy food in whatever way you are able and in whatever way will be accepted.

Could you share – or provide – a weekly meal out together at a restaurant that specializes in well-balanced fresh dishes? Great. Companionship combined with a delicious meal (or even snack) is a great way to help lift spirits, which in itself is therapeutic. Are you a cook? An invitation to supper at your place periodically could be good for the same reasons – emotional sustenance combined with physical nourishment. Is the patient too tired for companionship and the caregiver too tired or too unwilling to leave them? Maybe you can offer to do some fridge-stocking – a stack of individual portions of stew or soup – some to freeze, some to eat immediately -- small containers of bean and veggie salad, for example, or everything they'd need to quickly put together chicken wraps or fajitas with all the ingredients already cut, separated into little individual containers or compartments so they're ready for easy assembly. Or maybe you could provide nutritious snacks like hummus and cut-up vegetables, a container of fresh fruit salad with yogurt on the side, oat bars with nuts and dried fruits, whole grain muffins, creamy bean dip with pita wedges. The options are many, but keep in mind they need to be tailored to the circumstances, needs and tastes of the individual recipients.

Even if the patient turns down your special turnip-and-rhubarb fritters (though who wouldn't love these!), the offer itself is evidence of your love and support, so don't be offended if they say no thanks. This isn't about you. Maybe you could help by doing a market run for them once a week with a list they provide. It takes that chore off their shoulders, (and you could add a couple of additional healthy treats as nice secret-Santa-like gifts). One friend said that one of the most considerate gifts she could remember getting while her husband was dying of cancer was toilet paper and Tide, left on her doorstep by a thoughtful friend who had assumed she hadn't had time or focus enough to deal with those basic necessities while she was working fulltime and taking her husband to radiation and chemotherapy.

Even if you come up with what would ordinarily be the best possible nutrition for your friend, there may be other considerations to take into account. Depending upon the type of disease, the treatment and the individual, there can be a wide range of reactions – from zero changes in the patient's taste and appetite to everything tasting metallic or inducing nausea, to an aversion to certain textures or flavors, to suppressed appetite and trouble with digestion. It's sometimes hard to predict, even for the patient.

Years ago, Nancy offered a bowl of homemade oyster stew to Frank, a neighbor on chemo, who hadn't been able to keep anything down for days. Nothing appealed to him. In addition to the nausea he was experiencing, nothing tasted 'right.' The stew was a single serving of fresh-shucked Chesapeake Bay oysters stewed in a light cream broth laced with fresh parsley. She handed it over without comment in case it turned his stomach but he didn't want to seem ungrateful by refusing it. (Cow's milk and cream are notoriously difficult to digest sometimes, especially on a wonky stomach). It turned out to be not only the first thing Frank had been able to keep down for days, it was the first thing that he had truly enjoyed in weeks.

There is a wide range of appetites among people dealing with terminal illness. Some are curtailed by the specific disease or condition; some are impacted by medication. Some hinge on individual tastes and mental states. Nancy's father, who was diagnosed with bone cancer and told he most likely had 18 months to live (but who was still sailing two years later), was married to a good cook and enjoyed an evening cocktail (or two) and hearty meals until only a few weeks before he died. In contrast, Brad, who had never focused much on food, had little appetite. Emily, who believed that if properly nourished Brad could live a much longer, fuller life, decided it was her duty to try to feed him.

"I knew nutrition was not something that either Carla or Brad had any connection with — and I also thought it might have been a contributing factor in the cancer in the first place," Emily says now. "So I thought I was going to nourish him and help him come back from this."

She made nutritionally dense, easy-to-digest meals - butternut squash soups, risotto, fish, organic drinks — and gave them to Brad in small containers that he could freeze if he chose. He ate some, let some turn into science experiments in the refrigerator and threw some out. Carla, who knew and appreciated that Emily's effort was made out of love for them both, and who longed for her son to 'beat' the cancer, was nevertheless more realistic than Emily about the effect these edible care packages would have on the outcome.

"I knew Brad would do whatever he was going to do," she said, "And nagging him to eat properly wasn't going to change that. In fact, it was going to make us both miserable."

Emily isn't the only person to equate food with love, and to try to change the outcome with food. Some recipients will welcome this; for others it will be a nuisance. If you are part of the casserole brigade (and you know who you are), don't turn it into an unwholesome competition and don't force food on people.

Carla refused to nag her grown son. Taking a page from her friend's book, Emily quickly learned to make what Brad said he had enjoyed, adding something new to try each week. If he asked for something again, she made it; if not, she didn't and she never asked whether he had eaten what she had brought.

Offer to cook or bring food. If accepted, pay attention, listen closely, and watch. This is not about you saving the person or showing what a great cook you are. This is not about you converting the person to your way of life. This is about you helping without being pushy.

There are several things you need to know regarding food and a person who is terminally ill.

1. Appetite and activity are two things that decline in tandem, so the less active the person is the less they want and need to eat.

2. Certain drugs and conditions interact with certain foods, so be sure to find out what the person can and can't eat. (This is not necessarily the same list of foods the person will or won't eat.).

3. Tastes may change significantly due to medication, so even if the person is still hungry, their favorite foods may not taste good any more. Ask if there are things that now turn the person's stomach (it may include your signature tuna surprise that they'd always loved, so don't make it for them) and then ask if there are other things that may now appeal instead. And if they say thanks but no thanks, don't take it personally. This is not about you or your cooking

4. Unless there are plenty of people in the household who will also eat whatever you have made, offer small portions in individual containers. Large casseroles will not only be wasted, but can feel overwhelming to the person and their caregiver who may feel compelled to deal with them. Sometimes something simple and small is best.

DO's AND DON'T's

- DO offer to make a regular meal or meals so people can plan.

- DO coordinate with others if there are several members of the casserole brigade.

- DO ask if there are food restrictions before you cook or bring something.

- DO ask if there are favorite foods that would help the person regain appetite without causing difficulty in swallowing or digestion.

- DO include soups – chicken noodle, for example, has proven medicinal benefits – that are either easy to swallow or that have been pureed or made with fine-chopped vegetables.

- DON'T offer sodas, sugary treats, chemical-laden prepared foods, donuts, or other nutrition-deficient foods. They burden an already compromised system.

- DON'T lecture or criticize if the person wants only those things you consider unhealthy. This is still not about you.

- DON'T use too much salt, especially if the patient is taking steroids, which tend to add weight by making a person retain water. Salt can be added later if needed.

- DON'T nag.
- DON'T take offense if the person refuses your help – you can offer again at another time if you want. Take two refusals as final, however, unless the person or caregiver mentions how welcome your chicken noodle soup, or Swedish meatballs (or whatever) would be.

Bear in mind that you can't thrust help on someone. It's not about you wanting to help. It's about you actually helping a person on their terms, not necessarily on yours. (However, a request that you resupply a patient with cigarettes can legitimately be met with stony silence in our opinion.).

WHEN TO STOP FEEDING

Even with its benefits, chicken soup (aka Jewish penicillin) can't cure someone in the final stage of life. In fact, it *can* do more harm than good. Force-feeding a dying person can actually cause suffering – the very thing you are trying to avoid or alleviate. Forced feedings often leave the person feeling bloated and nauseated. Sometimes a bite or two is all they either want or need. The dying body cannot manage liquids normally. The lungs may be filling with fluid, and the body is adding to this fluid. In the case of cancer, for example, any introduced liquid may make the problem worse. Edema (swelling due to fluid) around tumors can increase pressure and pain while increased urine output necessitates more trips to the bathroom at a time when a person may already be weak and frail.

And yet…there is always an exception to the rule.

Sue remembers a woman at the hospice center who had been in a coma for the better part of two weeks. The distraught husband could not understand how she could 'go on living' without any food or drink. Then the night before she died, she woke up hungry, asking for ice cream, which the husband delightedly brought her. She 'ate the whole Dixie cup of vanilla ice cream,' the husband told Sue that evening. The couple had traveled extensively over the years and during that precious time when she was eating the ice cream, they reminisced, laughed and 'carried on' until she fell asleep and died only hours later.

"I recall how his face lit up when he told me this," Sue says. "This unexpected surge of energy is a very special time with a small window of shared opportunity."

Tube Feedings: If you are caring for someone who is receiving tube feedings the question invariably arises: how will you know when to decrease the amount or stop altogether? The big signal is: if the person becomes noticeably congested with frequent coughing during or immediately after feeding. Then the caregiver needs to stop, and try again in several hours. If the feeding will not drain through the feeding tube – assuming there is no clog in the apparatus – it could mean the contents from the last feeding remain in the stomach. If these symptoms do not change when you recheck 2-4 hours later, then it may be time to stop feedings at least for that day, then resume the next day. Forced tube feedings can result in lung issues such as shortness of breath, coughing and choking. It can also cause digestive and intestinal complaints such as nausea, vomiting and diarrhea. When in doubt seek the advice of the primary care physician or the guidance of a hospice care provider.

TIP: Allow the person to eat or drink whatever they wish as long as they are able to swallow and do not choke afterward.

THE DEHYDRATION QUESTION

The most common symptom of dehydration is a dry mouth. If the person is conscious, offer ice chips. Lip conditioner helps soothe dry lips. Encourage fluids as the dying person desires.

According to studies, at the very end of life, dehydration actually produces an endorphin that helps to keep us comfortable. Some people may take nothing by mouth for up to 14 days before death. The only discomfort is a dry mouth, which can be alleviated via mouth swabs, moist sponges and drops of water in the mouth.

What ultimately matters is the person's comfort and the love you and others offer them by whatever means.

Resources:
The Cancer-Fighting Kitchen: Nourishing, Big-Flavor Recipes for Cancer Treatment and Recovery by Rebecca Katz with Mt Edelson (Celestial Arts, Berkley)

One Bite at a Time, Revised: Nourishing Recipes for Cancer Survivors and Their Friends by Rebecca Katz and Mat Edelson (Celestial Arts, 2008).

Another good resource is The National Cancer Institute's online primer, **Eating Hints: Before, During and After Cancer Treatment**. (http://www.cancer.gov/cancertopics/coping/eatinghints/page1) You can also order a free copy.

Nutrition Therapy at Cancer Treatment Centers of America
http://www.cancercenter.com/complementary-alternative-
medicine/nutritional-
therapy.cfm?source=GOOGPHIL&channel=paid%20search&c=paid%20s
earch:Google:Google%20-
%20Eastern%20Core%20Terms%20New:General%3A+Cancer+Nutrition
:nutrition+for+cancer+patient:Exact

**Nutrition for the Person With Cancer During Treatment at American
Cancer Society**
http://www.cancer.org/Treatment/SurvivorshipDuringandAfterTreatment
/NutritionforPeoplewithCancer/NutritionforthePersonwithCancer/index

Nutrition for Children with Cancer at the American Cancer Center
http://www.cancer.org/Treatment/ChildrenandCancer/WhenYourChildH
asCancer/NutritionforChildrenwithCancer/index

**Nutrition In Cancer Care at the National Cancer Institute at the
National Institutes of Health**
http://www.cancer.gov/cancertopics/pdq/supportivecare/nutrition/Patie
nt/page1

Forks Over Knives, described by some as a vegan propaganda movie, purports
to actually cure cancer with this diet. It's worth seeing at least. The
cookbook is **Forks Over Knives: The Plant-Based Way to Health**
Gene Stone (Editor), Dr. T. Colin Campbell (Foreword), Dr. Caldwell
Esselstyn Jr. (Foreword)
http://www.forksoverknives.com/

The Dehydration Question

For more information on the effects of dehydration at the end of life, visit:

http://www.comfortcarechoices.com/index.php?option=com_content&vi
ew=article&id=139:is-dehydration-painful-at-the-end-of-life&catid=49:ask-
dr-webb&Itemid=81
http://www.medicalnewstoday.com/releases/137260.php
**http://abcnews.go.com/Health/Schiavo/story?id=531907&page=1#
.UFjLeY5OS-8**
http://www.growthhouse.org/mortals/mor11106.html

Chapter Eight

DRUGS ARE GOOD: SAY YES TO DRUGS

To give or not to give (narcotics)...that is ALWAYS the question.

Don't assume all terminal people need narcotics for pain. It depends on the disease and the person. For example, not all cancer causes pain. The type of cancer, the location, whether there are other chronic illnesses, and a person's individual tolerance to pain all enter into the equation. Additionally, other diseases that you may not think of as physically painful can cause pain. For example, Alzheimer's patients may experience pain; their decreased activity and appetite cause atrophy of the muscles putting a strain on the ligaments. In other words, there are many factors at play here. However, when there is pain, particularly chronic pain associated with a terminal disease, painkilling drugs can be a huge help.

Caregivers often feel ambivalent about the use of narcotics yet obviously want the best quality of life for their ill loved one. While it's agonizing to watch someone in pain suffer, there is often fear among caregivers and other loved ones that the narcotic will 'put them to sleep' (permanently). Before you allow your reason to run off with your fears, remember this: Narcotics are meant to be palliative. They are designed to soothe symptoms and pain, and are safe when given properly under a doctor's care. **Always** refer to your doctor or pharmacist for guidance and direction when administering narcotics to a loved one.

The questions many caregivers and family members ask when discussing the use of narcotics with physicians include: Will he be addicted to the morphine (or other prescribed narcotic)?

> Does taking it mean she is close to dying?
> If we give a narcotic will he be able to talk to us?
> How do you know that she's in pain and needs narcotics, especially toward the end when a person is in a coma-like state?
> Is the medicine making him sleep all the time?
> Will the narcotic put her in a coma?
> Will the narcotic kill him?
> Will the narcotic stop her breathing?
> If we start giving narcotics now, will they still work if the pain gets worse?

The questions emerge from good intentions coupled with genuine concerns. But they also stem from a lack of information and from fear fed by anti-addiction commercials or possibly the cryptic report of a celebrity dying from a drug overdose. We are not talking about drug addiction here, nor are we talking about overdosing someone. We are talking about using these very helpful drugs under a doctor's supervision for what they were designed for: pain control and symptom alleviation. Narcotics were designed to alleviate pain and suffering, period.

To calm fears, and benefit both you and your loved one, get informed. Read about narcotics online at: www.drugs.com or at the library. Talk with your physician. Talk with your local pharmacist. If your loved one is in a hospice program, talk with the nurse.

CLARIFYING THE PAIN TO INFORM THE PHYSICIAN

To clarify the amount and type of pain the person is experiencing, observe them, and ask questions. Often people in pain make general statements like:

> It hurts.
> I don't feel good.
> I ache all over.
> I feel terrible, bad or awful.
> I just don't feel good or right.

What do those statements actually say about the pain the person is having? Not much. The doctor will need more information in order to prescribe the correct medicine and the correct dosage. Being more specific can save days of trial and error to say nothing of time waiting for pain or other symptoms to subside. Your loved one will thank you – or if not, you will see a positive result, which in these cases can be as good as a thank you.

If the pain is new, ask the person the following questions:

> Where is the location of the pain?
> When did it start?
> How long does it last?
> What makes it worse? (An activity? Eating? Drinking? Moving in a specific way?)
> What improves the pain? (A position, perhaps?)
> What is its intensity?

There are different types of pain and different types of medicine used to alleviate it. Determining the type of pain will help narrow down the type of drug best needed to assure faster relief.

Acute pain comes on suddenly for a limited duration, such as a cut, burn or accident. This is not usual in terminal illness. However if a person has bone metastasis and experiences a spontaneous bone fracture, there is acute pain obviously in need of immediate medical attention.

Chronic pain lasts longer than acute pain – three to six months – and is usually associated with a terminal illness. (Headaches, backaches and pain from injury are examples of non-terminal chronic pain). Chronic pain can be debilitating and can bring on anxiety and depression. Chronic pain can come and go in intensity several times a day.

Somatic pain comes from skin, muscles, bone, joints, tendons and ligaments. It is dull or aching in nature, but can be stabbing at times, like an arthritic flare up. Somatic pain can be caused by inflammation from a fluid-producing tumor or from internal bleeding due to tumor damage. NSAID's (non-steroidal anti-inflammatory drugs like aspirin, ibuprofen or acetaminophen) can be very effective. Steroids are often used to reduce tissue edema (swelling from fluid) in conditions such as brain tumors or tumors in the spine.

Visceral Pain (soft tissue) refers to damage of the organs i.e. heart, lungs, kidney, bladder, uterus. It feels like squeezing, pressure from distention (as in liver or ovarian cancers), spasms or cramping. This pain can also be caused from constipation, a potential side effect of narcotics. This type of pain can cause referred pain in the back or pelvis from pressure of the enlarged organs. Narcotics (sometimes coupled with a stool softener or laxative) are generally effective for this type of pain.

Nerve pain is damage that feels much like 'pins and needles.' People usually describe numbness, burning, tingling, pinching or shooting pains from such causes as carpel tunnel syndrome, sciatica or tumors pushing on a nerve (as in cancer of the spine). Nerve pain can be caused by inflammation, pressure or infection. There are specific medicines that can be taken along with narcotics for nerve pain.

Once the type of pain is determined, it is very helpful to find out the intensity. This will help the doctor prescribe a prudent but effective starting dose. To determine the intensity, first ask the person where they would rate the pain on a scale of one to ten – ten being the worst it has ever been. If you believe they are low-balling the number, study their face. Sometimes it tells more than their words, particularly if you are dealing with a stoic. The link below will take you to the Wong-Baker Pain Scale website. It illustrates facial expressions and associates them with relative amounts of pain the person is suffering. http://www.wongbakerfaces.org/

Other factors can influence the amount of pain a person feels, including:

Mood changes: such as anxiety, fear, depression or irritability.
Fatigue,
Sleeplessness
Decrease in activity, so there is more focus on the pain
Disability

DOSAGE IS ONLY A NUMBER; DIFFERENT STROKES FOR DIFFERENT FOLKS

Bear in mind that pain is subjective in the body of the sufferer. For instance some women would rather give birth than have a root canal. Some people howl over a broken toe, while others could have a toe amputated and say nothing. You probably have an idea which of these best describes your loved one.

A potentially complicating factor in determining proper dose to control pain is a history of drug and/or alcohol abuse in the person, (which is something the physician needs to be informed of). Their body may have built up a tolerance for alcohol or drugs over time and need higher doses to feel even a little relief. Additionally, if the liver is damaged it may not be functioning well enough to properly process the narcotic in what would be considered a 'normal' dose, necessitating higher doses to achieve any relief at all – as with a 24-year-old man who was admitted to the hospice center at which Sue worked.

He had been diagnosed with a rare lung disease and was in the end stages. He used two oxygen concentrators and wore two nasal cannula (tubes) in his nose to deliver the oxygen. He was also taking morphine through a continuous drip in his arm. The morphine was in a small cassette in a fanny pack. The hourly dose he received was 800 milligrams an hour. Eight HUNDRED milligrams an hour is enough to wipe out the entire hospice staff on duty at the time. And yet his respirations were still high at 38-48 breaths a minute. (The normal rate of respirations for an adult at rest is 15-20 per minute). In addition to being used for pain, morphine can help alleviate "air hunger." Because his liver was damaged and not processing the morphine normally, this unbelievably high dose was not helping his breathing. But it was also not bringing him closer to coma or death. This young man was alert, able to communicate (though barely

due to what amounted to continuous panting) and was able to walk very slowly to the
bathroom on his own.

This dosage was an extremely rare situation, but our point is: Each person is individual, as is their personal history, their tolerance to a narcotic and therefore their dosage. A person's individual internal chemistry also affects how much narcotic as well as the type of narcotic is needed i.e. some people tolerate and get relief from one type that others would not be able to tolerate.

Many try to do without narcotics. They view the use of narcotics as the sign of weakness so they tough it out until they can't stand the pain any more, or they have a fear of becoming addicted. However, frequent, regularly scheduled doses of narcotic are more effective than waiting to take something when the pain is out of control. Additionally, the scheduled approach usually results in less total medication being taken. Most opioids come in both short and long-acting formulations. The specifics of the prescribed narcotic are something to be discussed with the physician in the individual person's case.

Despite all the factors that can affect the dosage needed for a specific individual, caregivers sometimes focus on the number of milligrams of narcotic that has been prescribed. Sometimes, worried that they might be overdosing the person, they think: Maybe I'll just try half a dose. Or I'll just give it when he asks for it, which can set up a cycle – the person feels their caregiver's reluctance and then tries to be 'good' by not requesting pain medication until they cannot bear the pain any longer.

Don't focus on the number of milligrams your loved one is taking. The narcotic dose needed is whatever it takes to get the pain (and possibility other symptoms) under control at the level at which the pain is acceptable to them. End of story.

ONLY GIVE MEDICATION AS PRESCRIBED BY THE PHYSICIAN. Do not hesitate to call the doctor for clarification.

Sometimes the person actively resists narcotics. They may be worried that narcotics will impair their ability to control what life is left to them, or will impair their ability to remain completely lucid, or will encourage them to give up.

In Sue's hospice experience, men resist the use of narcotics more frequently than women. It seems to be wrapped around the issue of control. Whether men are consciously taught that competition, taking charge and powering through to win against whatever adversary they encounter is their responsibility, whether it is a mandate they absorb from society or whether it is in their DNA is the old nature/nurture question that is fairly useless to debate here. Maybe they believe they will seem weak if they succumb to the use of narcotics. For others, feeling the symptoms equals being alive. Whatever the reason, the fact is, men seem more prone than women to resisting narcotics that could help them. Often, the more high-powered a man has been in his life – a take-charge guy, a physical guy, a man who has been accustomed to calling the shots in his life – the more he resists medication. By the time a man has reached the end of life through a disease, he has usually suffered many losses: a job, his role in the family, stamina, appetite, perhaps every vice large or small that he's held dear. As a result, he wants to retain control of what remains within his grasp. Letting go – of anything – is not something for which he's been programmed. Dylan Thomas's poem for his dying father is a watchword for many: "Do not go gentle in that good night. Rage, rage against the dying of the light." (Of course, we all, on some level, rage against the dying of our life, but we're talking here about easing the inevitable passage).

Some resist because they worry they will become addicted. Nancy's father, who had been no stranger to strong drink throughout his life, still worried in the last months that using narcotics would mean he would become addicted to them, which for him would have meant a stain on his character. Nancy and her brother refrained from saying: You won't have time to become addicted. Instead, they assured him that being comfortable and as pain-free as possible was a GOOD thing and a way to take what joy he could from each day. Which was true. Once reassured, he acquiesced, which made the time he had here easier both on him and on those who loved him. It is very difficult to watch someone suffer, especially if there is a means of alleviating that suffering.

For many people, the mere idea of taking a narcotic can trigger a fear of hastening death. As a result, they will continue to suffer with the symptoms of their disease – pain, nausea, vomiting or shortness of breath – convinced that this is their form of raging against the dying of the light. It may be their form of raging, but it may not produce the desired extension of their time here.

Mr. Mercer came to the hospice center seeking 'comfort care,' but on his arrival at the center, he made it clear to the staff that in his case, comfort care would not include narcotics. Certain that pain medication would impair his ability to control his own life, he resisted. He was determined to 'be himself,' make his own choices, and not let opiates take over. But he was obviously struggling and in extreme pain.

The staff felt miserable. They periodically made an effort to convince him to accept medication to at least ease if not eradicate the pain. He continued to refuse, determined not to succumb to what he imagined pain medication would do to his faculties, to his ability to experience life, and perhaps because he feared it would unnaturally hasten his death. But while he was suffering, his family was suffering, too.

Ellen, one of the hospice nurses, sat down at his bedside to see if she could gently persuade him to at least try medication. At that moment a spasm of pain convulsed him. When it had subsided, he dragged himself to a sitting position; the two studied each other silently for a moment then Ellen spoke.

"There comes a time to let go," she told him. "If that's something you've not done too often, it won't be easy now."

He shook his head. No.

The staff had never seen a conviction so strong. Many families have subjected their dying loved ones to restrictions in the name of advocating for them. Some are enforcing their loved one's stated wishes, others are worried about the loss of the person's clarity, consciousness, and ability to be present for their family. Regardless of the motive, it is a hard road to travel for everyone – for the suffering person, for those who love them and must stand by helplessly, watching them suffer, and for the staff, whose job and wish it is to alleviate suffering as much as is humanly possible.

Mr. Mercer didn't mean to add to the emotional burden of his wife and two sons. He simply believed that this was the best way for him to fight his own death to the end. His wife and sons respected his wishes. Their respect for his choice and their devoted love, while miserable at his pain, helped sustain the staff. But as Mr. Mercer's mental clarity waned, the staff began to talk more with his family about the benefits of alleviating his pain.

"The sooner we can learn to have less control," Ellen told them, "the easier it can be in the final moment."

Aware that the staff sees death first hand, over and over again, and knowing that he was now unable to decide for himself, Mr. Mercer's family finally agreed to start pain medication. Unfortunately, because his body lacked a stabilizing back load of medication, which would have stabilized his pain, there was not enough time for the narcotics to control it completely before his death. However, he was certainly more comfortable than he had been in the two hours prior to receiving medication.

Ellen was impressed by how Mr. Mercer's wife and sons were not only able to honor his wishes but they were able to recognize when to go beyond his wishes. In her opinion, "they really pulled it together for him in the end."

When she has encountered men with an anti-narcotic mindset who would benefit from some chemically aided relief, Sue acknowledges their goal of trying to preserve some control in their current circumstances. Then she explains that not taking a prescribed narcotic to ease breathing and mitigate pain may inadvertently hasten death rather than prolong life. For example, at end stage emphysema the heart is pumping harder with the depleted oxygen levels in the blood stream while the lungs are also working harder to take in air. The struggle affects all the organs and systems in the body, creating tension that results in physical exhaustion. A prescribed narcotic can ease the shortness of breath and thereby ease the tension, which positively affects the quality (and in some cases the amount) of the time the person has left.

"When I've talked with men who resist taking the narcotics that could help them, I explain what their resistance may be doing to them physically," Sue says. "Generally, they're grateful and their response has been, 'I hadn't looked at it that way.' When a skeptic tries a narcotic they feel some relief."

Ultimately the person is in the driver's seat – it's their hands, or, if the person is physically unable to call the shots, it's in the hands of their designated medical proxy, which is why it's a good idea to have one. As a caregiver, it can be anguishing to watch a loved one suffer, but this time is about them; we have to accept *their* choice.

The mission of hospice (and of course each caregiver) is to relieve suffering, to ease dis-ease, and to help those navigating an anguishing physical, emotional and spiritual labyrinth. Many people believe that calling in hospice is the sign that all hope for recovery is gone. Often it is, but certainly not always.

"I always say to try hospice on, and see how it fits with your goals," Sue says. "Live with it awhile since it can always be returned. Suffering can show up unannounced, demanding attention; hospice is a possible solution."

Nancy's mother-in-law had called hospice in a full year before she died. After a few weeks, she rallied, checked out of the program and went back to life as she had been living it. A year later, when she was clearly failing very fast, the family called the service in again. This time, she had only two weeks before she breathed her last, comfortably, in her own home.

A WORD ABOUT SIDE EFFECTS

All drugs have side effects, including the over the counter drugs most of us have taken at one time or another. Have you ever read the list of side effects for aspirin? Opioids/narcotics are no exception. Potential side effects include constipation, nausea, and vomiting, rash, dry mouth, which may go away after a few doses. Each person's body can react differently to *any* drug. Each person's medical history can influence on the body's response to narcotics as well. Call your doctor for medical advice about side effects and how to alleviate them.

Despite the flippant subtitle to this chapter, let us be clear here. We are not pushing drugs. We are advocating a thoughtful, informed and caring consideration of what prescribed narcotics can do to ease a person's suffering by mitigating or alleviating pain and symptoms.

Chapter Nine

WHEN TO CALL THE PROFESSIONALS

CALL IN HOSPICE WHEN:

Aggressive treatment is no longer effective OR when a decision has been made to stop treatment.

You can no longer assist the person out of bed.

Appetite is reduced to sips and bites.

Naps become longer and longer.

There is increased confusion, lethargy and disorientation.

Tension between patient and caregiver, caregiver and family members hangs like a fog in the home.

MANY CAREGIVERS PUT OFF CALLING HOSPICE BECAUSE THEY THINK:

That hospice is a place that we've tried to avoid; we wanted to orchestrate care at home.

That hospice means they have failed.

That hospice means everyone has given up hope.

That it means you have let your loved one down somehow; you don't love them the same way you did or the way you feel you should.

That hospice is only used at the very end of life, so death is all that is left.

That hospice hastens death.

That the person will not have the option to be resuscitated.

That hospice is only for people with cancer.

That it's too expensive.

NONE IS TRUE

HOSPICE FACTS:

Hospice, originally a shelter or lodging for pilgrims, travelers and others in need, is about quality of life – promoting and preserving quality – as well as about physical comfort. Hospice care is designed to get symptoms under control. Once that happens, often the person will want to eat, get out of bed or have visitors since control of symptoms makes them feel better. At this point some caregivers question whether the call to hospice was premature or necessary, though improvement should in itself be seen as a positive outcome.

The person – or you, if you have the legal power – can sign out of a hospice program at any time, whether the person wants to try new treatment or simply changes his or her mind. As we've already noted, Nancy's mother-in-law had hospice for a while, then signed out and lived contentedly and relatively symptom-free with her live-in caregiver for more than a year more before she died.

Hospice does have graduates, if their quality of life is such that the person may now feel as though they can travel, go see someone they were afraid they'd never see again, visit a place they'd always wanted to see, try an alternative protocol.

WHAT YOU SHOULD KNOW ABOUT CALLING IN HOSPICE:

1. Anyone can make an inquiry to hospice. Two physicians, generally the primary care doctor and the hospice physician, are responsible for determining the illness as terminal, i.e. with a life expectancy of six months or less. A hospice representative can make a house visit and help determine if hospice care is appropriate; the representative will get the paper work started.

2. Be aware that calling in hospice may be an extremely unpopular decision with friends and other family members, especially among those who have not been active in the person's daily care. Many believe hospice represents all of the things mentioned above – a death sentence, giving up. Some will lash out in fear, frustration, anger, or disdain. A calm, rational discussion with the objecting party can help defuse emotional resistance to the idea. Others will resist vehemently. This is why is it helpful to have a discussion about this impending death sooner rather than later as mentioned earlier. If the resisting party or parties still don't get it, consider encouraging them to participate in care. Firsthand experience often illustrates the fact that hospice is a reasonable, even desirable step to take. It can also illustrate the fact that the person needs more assistance than is apparent in a short visit. (A person with a strong will can summon amazing energy to present well for a visitor, then lapse into exhaustion and reliance as soon as the visitor is gone). A hospice social worker can be crucial in thwarting arguments and hostility between resistant relatives or friends and the primary caregiver when hospice is called in. If needed, the hospice staff can also act as the 'bad guys' who set the rules such as visiting restrictions, like the number of people or the length of stay.

3. The person can still receive CPR if needed even if they're in hospice. The Do Not Resuscitate (DNR) order needs to be in place before a hospice worker will not attempt to resuscitate.

Some people in hospice want resuscitation attempted. This may sound like a contradiction – and in some ways, it is, but it is decidedly not giving up. When hospice began in the US in 1974, many hospices created a rule requiring a person to have a Do Not Resuscitate (DNR) order to become a hospice patient. Years later, Medicare put a stop to that practice, so now the choice is yours, but there is a calculation to be made as to whether it will painfully (physically) prolong an already difficult passage, or whether in a very few cases, it could be the last-ditch effort that allows someone like Annie's mother to let go without guilt.

Thirty-one-year-old Annie had been battling cancer for several years, but was obviously coming down to the end. Two days after she came to the hospice center, Sue noticed something was different.

"It was nothing specific we could point to," Sue says, but the staff agreed that something was off. Perhaps it was the frequent trips to the bathroom, the daily increases of pain medicine, the dark circles developing under her eyes, the increasing naps, all subtle, but we suspected it added up to something bigger."

Earlier that day, the doctor suggested cutting back on the Total Parenteral Nutrition (TPN), due to the possibility that it could be feeding the tumors. TPN administered through an IV and is packed with carbohydrates, proteins, lipids, and electrolytes. Annie's mother refused.

"Cutting back on TPN will make her weaker," she replied. "She can't keep anything down. She needs nourishment. She's handled tougher situations than this and she always bounces back. We just need patience to get through this."

The staff was not convinced, yet respected a mother's determination to keep her only child as long as she could. Annie did not have a Do Not Resuscitate (DNR) order in place, which meant that should her heart or breathing stop, there would be an attempt to resuscitate her.

Later that evening while making rounds, the aide noticed Annie's lips were white and she felt clammy.

"When I entered the room Annie's hospital gown was soaked, and she was not responding," Sue says. "She did not move or open her eyes; something was happening fast. I asked Annie's parents to step outside of their daughter's room to talk."

Sue told Annie's parents what she was seeing.

"Her face is white, she loosing color and I want your permission to call 911," I told them. "This may not be anything, but I do not want to wait until Annie stops breathing to make the call!" I believed then that Annie was dying, but I also knew that her mother would not let her go without the last fight she could wage to keep her here and I wanted to honor her wishes."

After calling 911, Sue called the ER to give a report on Annie. The ER nursed hollered to a co-worker, "Keep that bay open, hospice is sending someone."

"In the background I heard the protest: "Why is hospice sending someone? IT'S HOSPICE!"" Sue remembers. "They were medical professionals, but it appeared that they didn't know that there is a procedure for this circumstance."

Several hours later Annie's father returned to the hospice center to gather her things.

"You were right to send her to the hospital," he told Sue. "We're really glad you did!"

Annie had been transferred to the intensive care unit and spent a week there before returning home. She survived for several more weeks. The second time her heart stopped, the paramedics were unable to revive her. As searing as this loss was, her mother's grief was not complicated with the guilt of not having tried everything.

Many EMT's and hospital staff don't realize that being in hospice does not preclude being resuscitated. Also, even a professional coming into such a situation does not necessarily have the full picture of the people and the history involved. As we said, each person's death is individual; the timing and circumstances surrounding that death are enormously personal, and no one has a calendar on another person's life. Sue's frustration with these EMT's was born of advocacy for the patient, her first priority – and of her knowledge that what Annie's parents wanted was legal and was also something that they believed was a moral necessity both for themselves and for Annie. BUT it's important to remember that while CPR can sometimes restore heart and lung function, it does not have any effect on the disease that the person is dying from. CPR performed on an already fragile body could crush bones and make that last passage even more painful than it would have been otherwise had the person be allowed to simply stop.

WHAT EXACTLY IS HOSPICE?

Hospice is an organization, usually not for profit, usually community-based with fulltime and part-time paid staff as well as volunteers who can make home visits. Their mission is to ease the last weeks and days of a dying person. A hospital's mission is to heal, or improve a person's situation; generally, hospital staff is not necessarily trained in palliative care (though some are).

"The last memory of my father is of him gasping for air," says Linda a nurse. "That's how he lived with lung cancer, short of breath and gasping for air. He had been in the hospital for six weeks. One afternoon, my supervisor tracked me down at a patient's home. Not knowing how to sugarcoat it, she relayed the message she received from the hospital: they said I should come right away. Nurses understand the real meaning behind that statement."

Linda hurried to be with her father at the moment of his death, but arrived too late.

"I walked into my father's room to find the bed stripped and my father's body gone. To my utter astonishment, nobody, not one person tried to stop me from entering his room despite the fact that he had been in the hospital for six weeks and I had visited daily."

Linda was astonished at the seeming coldness and disconnectedness of the staff, who had simply let her walk in expecting to be with her father during his last moments. No one had made any attempt to gently tell her he had gone. It was, in her view, unfeeling.

"He died in the hospital," she says. "He died alone, gasping for air."

Twenty years later, Linda's mother was diagnosed with cancer. By then, Linda was a hospice nurse and had seen firsthand how much different hospice could help make the experience for both the dying and for the family. Her father's death in the hospital had been impersonal, clinical, while a death assisted by hospice can be more connected, more personal, and more satisfying for those left behind.

"I wanted hospice care for her," Linda says. "And working in hospice, I understand the benefits of an early admission. But Mom fought hospice. 'That's your thing not mine!' she told me." She felt I was pushing. Once she recognized she couldn't get well though, she said, "It's time. I'm ready for hospice." Initially, Mom signed into the hospice home care program and moved into my home. This had an emotional impact on me. I was more than her caregiver. I was her daughter, and I preferred that role [to the dual caregiver/daughter roles she had been playing]. Mom was in the program for a week when she experienced some breathing difficulties and wanted to be transferred to the hospice center."

The differences between her father's death in the hospital and the palliative care her mother received in hospice meant not only that Linda's mother suffered less, but that Linda, who yearned for her mother to have as easy a passage as possible, suffered less too.

WHERE IS HOSPICE PROVIDED?

Hospice care can be provided at home, in a hospital, nursing home, assisted living facility and hospice facility. Wherever the person lives is where hospice can be provided.

Many nursing homes or assisted living facilities have contracts with local hospice providers, so check with the facility. If it does not have a current contract with a hospice provider, ask if they would consider obtaining one. If the facility offers 'comfort care' and 'morphine for pain' find out exactly what that means. Will the needed morphine be given around the clock or is it given only when the person asks for it? Will it be given immediately or will the person have to wait while the pain increases?

Some questions to ask a facility offering self-described comfort care:

1. Is the medical director or any of their other physicians certified in Hospice and Palliative Care? A Hospice and Palliative certification recognizes specialized knowledge, skills and experiences that promote optimal services and management of symptoms. Hospice professionals are trained to achieve the best quality of life for the patient and their family.

2. Are any of the staff nurses certified in Hospice and Palliative Care?

3. Does comfort care provide proper pain and/or symptom management?

4. Does comfort care include relief from suffering in spiritual, emotional and psychological areas?

5. Does comfort care include bereavement services? If so, what is their training and background for this service?

6. Are there volunteers available for companionship?

7. Do they have staff members who can sit vigil so a person does not die alone?

WHAT DOES HOSPICE COVER?

Physician services
Nursing care
Home health aide services
Counseling, social workers, chaplains and spiritual counselors
Bereavement services
Volunteers, end-of-life doulas, who support the dying and their family much like a birthing doula assists in labor
Physical, speech and occupational therapy
Medical Equipment, (hospital beds, commodes, wheel chairs)
Medical Supplies (dressings, catheters, syringes)
Medication
Respite care to give the primary caregiver a rest
Hospice staff is available via phone 24/7, which can be extremely comforting, especially when things happen in the middle of the night; you can get guidance and direction immediately without the anxiety of waiting until morning.

HOWEVER, hospice DOES NOT provide 24-hour care at home. (Some people assume they do). When a person is at home under hospice care, hospice can bring in outside people for adjunct care, and they are available via telephone.

HOSPICE CO-PAY

For many years a hospice program could charge up to but not exceed $5.00 for each prescription and 5% for inpatient respite care for caregivers. However, since these fees may change, ask your local hospice how they handle the Medicare co-pay guidelines. For patients under 65, most private health insurance companies follow the Medicare Hospice benefit guidelines, but check with your insurance to find out exactly what is covered. A hospice representative can also seek out and provide this information.

How long are benefits provided? As of this writing, benefits cover two periods of 90 days each followed by an unlimited number of periods of 60 days each. At any time you can decide to stop receiving hospice and return to other Medicare benefits (provided of course that the patient qualifies). The person can continue to receive hospice care after six months as long as the doctor recertifies that he or she is terminally ill. The hospice agency will describe benefits available in detail and give out copies to read and keep with you.

A POINT WORTH MENTIONING:

Hospice programs provide all the mentioned services for the admitting diagnosis. So, what does that mean, and how does that translate to your particular situation? If, for example, a person has been an insulin dependent diabetic for many years and has come into a hospice program with a diagnosis of lung cancer, the insulin will continue to be paid for as it always has, but all medicine needed for the lung cancer, such as narcotics, anti-depressants, anti-anxiety, anti-inflammatory, laxatives and medicine for secretions will be covered by hospice. Or, say a person has used a motorized wheelchair due to severe rheumatoid arthritis, but has developed pancreatic cancer. The payment of the wheelchair (if not owned outright) would not be covered by hospice. A person may have several conditions simultaneously and may continue taking the medications for these conditions such as heart disease. Hospice, however, does not pay for any medication that is not related to the terminal (admitting) illness.

ALZHEIMER'S, DEMENTIA, DEBILITY, OH MY

A person with Alzheimer's or dementia can live a long time, depending on their physical fitness. Often those caring for Alzheimers sufferers do not consider hospice care for respite or as an alternative to the 24/7 care that caregivers must give. However the daily stress of dealing with repetition, wandering and aggression can leave a caregiver desperate for relief. Hospice may be an option.

As of this writing, the Medicare guidelines for determining disease progression and consideration for terminal illness are as follows:

1. Unable to ambulate without assistance
2. Unable to dress without assistance
3. Unable to bathe without assistance
4. Incontinence of bladder and bowel, constant or intermittent
5. 10% weight loss in past six months
6. Speech is limited to six or fewer intelligible words
7. Unable to sit without props/assistance
8. Can no longer smile
9. Aspiration pneumonia in last 12 months
10. Recurrent kidney infections
11. Septicemia, a life-threatening infection in the blood
12. Decubitus ulcers (bed sores), multiple and advanced

DEBILITY

General debility in the elderly is the result of a lifetime of wear and tear on the body. Sometimes people die from natural causes like completion of the aging process, which is a natural consequence of living. Hospice is not reserved solely for intractable pain, respiratory distress, or restlessness. Death is not that particular. After all we are all moving toward impending death.

Here are some guidelines for debility:

If a person:

Is in a state of weakness, where everything is an effort.
Has repeated infections such as pneumonia, flu, urinary tract infections.
Has no energy, or interest in life.
Is perpetually fatigued.
Has no appetite, experiences weight loss, recurrent aspiration of food or stomach secretions (or both) into the lungs, which indicates difficulty in swallowing.
Is unsteady, has experienced recent falls.
Is confused, forgetful, anxious, agitated, has experienced a change in the level of consciousness.
Is having hallucinations.
Is retaining fluid even while taking diuretics.
Had nausea, vomiting, and/or diarrhea that either return quickly or do not resolve easily.
Has made multiple trips to the ER for the same issue/illness.

If a person has a history of:
COPD
Congestive Heart Failure
Diabetes
Renal Failure
Neurological disorders, such as Parkinson's, stroke.

Hospice can help the caregiver navigate through the body's decline, providing support for body, mind and spirit.

Resources:

National Hospice PCO
http://www.nhpco.org/templates/1/homepage.cfm

The Hospice Association of America
228 7th street SE
Washington DC 20003
1-202-546-4759
www.hospice-america.org

State Hospice org to find a hospice program in your area
1-800-854-3402
http://www.hospicedirectory.org/cm/about/state_hospice

Medicare
1-800-633-4227
http://www.medicare.gov/help-and-resources/contact/contact-medicare.html

End Stage Indicators
http://www.montgomeryhospice.org/health-professionals/end-stage-indicators

Chapter Ten

HOW TO SIT WITH THE ACTIVELY DYING

Dying cannot be compartmentalized. The process doesn't occur in any sequential order. It can't be pigeonholed into a neat series of symptoms that follow one on the other – first this happens, then that – so you know exactly what stage the person has reached and can brace yourself or plan accordingly. Dying is a unique and different experience for each individual.

There is, however, a series of common occurrences a person in the process of taking his or her leave from this life may experience that you, sitting at the bedside of a loved one, might witness. You could see one or two of them, or you could see all or none of them. But, we've seen that having an idea of what *could* occur can be a comfort to those standing by, particularly if this is your first close-up experience with death. An idea of what you might witness helps to lesson fears and anxieties, and allows you to be truly present without worrying about what may or may not happen along the way.

COLD HANDS COLD FEET

The hands and feet of the dying become cool or sometimes very cold to the touch. Adding three more blankets doesn't help. In fact, most dying people dislike the weight of blankets and even sheets on their bodies. Sometimes they pluck at their clothes or try to strip off everything, including their clothes, a tendency that families can find disturbing. These two things are simply more symptoms of the person's preparation for leaving.

TIP: If the person continually removes the covers, offer them a sheet and avoid drafts.

The coolness of the person's extremities often comes and goes; the hands can be very cold with a dusky bluish color, then an hour later, feel warm with the return of natural color. The pulse in the wrist may wax and wane from being a strong, occasionally bounding pulse, to a weak and barely palpable one. The soles of the feet can turn a deep purple with purple discoloration at the knees or scattered in the legs with subsequent return to normal. If the person has an elevated temperature, the extremities will be warm without mottling even though the circulation is changing. All these things are evidence that the circulatory system is declining and shutting down. This can come and go for hours, days or weeks before death, depending on the condition of the heart.

The declining circulation can show up as a bluish or light gray hue of the earlobes, around the mouth or the nail beds. The entire face often has a pasty ashen look and at times a bronze (looks like a weird tan) if the liver is involved in the disease. As death approaches, the color can change to a waxy, yellow cast.

YES, VIRGINIA, THEY CAN HEAR YOU

As the normal metabolic changes occur in the body, the person may spend more hours of the day asleep than awake and be difficult to arouse. They may be uncommunicative or unresponsive. However, Sue says she and many other hospice workers believe that hearing may be the last sense to go. Over and over again, we've seen a dying person demonstrate some awareness – a hand squeeze, a smile, or mouthing words in response to the words of a loved one, especially.

One striking demonstration of this came with one of Sue's patients, an elderly woman in a coma-like state at the hospice center. She had been completely unresponsive for several days. Despite her seemingly vegetative state, her son visited faithfully every day after work. He talked to her about his day and about her grandchildren, easy conversations that he would have had with her at the kitchen table. After a week of this, she suddenly opened her eyes when he came to visit one day. Naturally, he was very excited; he began to recap some of his conversations of the previous week. Smiling, she was able to relay parts of them back to him. He was stunned.
"I didn't know what to do when I came..." he began.
"So you talked my ear off," she said, finishing his sentence for him.

TIP: Speak to them from the heart, tell them you love them, and you will miss them. Sitting by the bed, speaking in a soft, soothing tone can be very comforting to both of you.

This is also a warning not to say anything in front of an apparently unresponsive person that you wouldn't say to their wide-awake face. Though they may not give any indication that they can hear, an unresponsive person can become restless or anxious when others are having a conversation in the room. Maybe they are frustrated that they can't participate, or perhaps what they hear is disturbing – siblings squabbling over money, over funeral arrangements or which clothes to 'lay them out in,' for example.

TIP: Do not argue with other visitors in their presence. The bedside is not the place to have ongoing debates about casket choices. (You'd be surprised how often this occurs!) It's also not the time to get off your chest whatever's been bugging you all these years. There are friends, priests, shrinks and bartenders for that. While you're at the bedside, let it go.

Also, don't talk about a family member or a friend the dying person may be concerned about unless there is also a plan in place for taking care of that person. Without a plan, the dying may be worried about leaving – who will take care of that person? What will become of them? By having a plan in place and telling the dying person about that plan, they can leave with some confidence.

THE FACE TELLS ALL

A person who is so minimally responsive that there's very little reaction to repositioning an arm, for example, will demonstrate feelings with facial expressions. It may be a grimace, it may be a furrowed brow, or their eyes may suddenly open wide in reaction to discomfort.

Even if the dying person is partially responsive, he or she may appear to be looking through you instead of focusing on you. They may focus on the ceiling, tracking back and forth as if they are watching something or someone. Ask them: Who do you see? What do you see?

Often the responsive dying talk about deceased relatives. They may tell you someone has visited them, or is sitting at the foot of the bed or in a chair in the room. They may tell you about conversations they have had with them in the room. You may even watch your loved one talking with someone you don't see. (This creeps some people out, but it's perfectly normal, it happens all the time, so try not to let it bother you). One friend of Nancy's was sitting by her 90-year-old father's bedside listening to a conversation he was having with someone who, as far as the daughter could see, was not in the room. It was apparently a good conversation, and he stopped in mid-sentence, and died with a smile on his face. A shock, certainly, but a peaceful end to his life.

TIP: If you witness such conversations, don't interrupt. Just let it happen.

TIP: Pay attention. Even if you believe the person is hallucinating, don't try to pull the dying back into your reality. What they are seeing and/or hearing could be a window into the next step in life or it could be a hallucination. Whichever it is, there's no point in trying to change it. For those who believe there is (or who accept that there could be) something beyond this corporeal life, the visions and manifestations of the dying can be consoling, revealing and wonderful to the observer. These things can be gifts that the dying person gives to those who remain. For those who believe it's only a hallucination, what exactly would be the point of trying to argue the person out of it? To make you feel better? Remember, this is not about you.

TAKE A BREATH

One of the most agonizing experiences while sitting at the bedside of a dying person can be listening to their breathing. Why? Because the breathing is all over the place. It can be shallow, fast, irregular, noisy, labored and abnormally slow. The most distressing is the Cheyne-Stokes respiratory pattern, which occurs because oxygen uptake is diminishing and waste products are building up in the organs. This pattern consists of irregular shallow breaths that slow to periods of no breathing at all for anywhere from 5 to 30 seconds followed by a deep, loud intake of breath. Sitting at the bedside, you may believe your loved one has gone, especially if the apnea (non-breathing) lasts longer than 30 seconds. As you begin to deal with what you think is the end, the person startles you (or scares the crap out of you) with a deep intake of breath. Breathing patterns can change several times in an hour, which makes it emotionally draining to wait and listen and keep wondering over and over if you've just heard the last one.

Congestion is another stressor for those sitting at a bedside. Here, mouth breathing is common, which amplifies the gurgling sounds coming from the lungs. Reading the expression on the face is crucial. No matter how loud the congestion may sound, typically, if the face appears peaceful, the congestion is more disturbing to the onlooker than to the dying person.

Wheezing may come and go on either intake or exhale. The wheezing may be accompanied by moaning. Again, watch the facial expression; moaning does not necessarily mean there is a problem or there is discomfort. Sometimes moaning is a comfort mechanism, as we sometimes do during a stomachache. Moaning can feel good.

CAREGIVER TIP: Gravity is a non-invasive action that can help drain congestion. Raise the head with several pillows, elevate the head of the bed if possible or raise it if it's a hospital bed. Repositioning the person onto a side can provide comfort. If they don't settle after repositioning, try another position or return to the previous one. Sometimes, medication may decrease the congestion or calm rapid breathing. Oxygen can sometimes be a comfort, but it does not prolong life because the person's physical ability to use oxygen is diminishing.

CAREGIVER TIP: Using a fan to circulate air may provide comfort

DO NOT LIE IN BED NEXT TO AN ACTIVELY DYING PERSON

Why not? Think of a time when you felt physically ill, the worse flu in your life, for example. It was so uncomfortable, so unbearable you felt like you were dying. You had aches and weakness in parts of the body you had never even thought about until then. You were curled, helpless, into a fetal position, every inch of skin hypersensitive to the touch, your concentration totally on waiting for this to pass. Or imagine a severe migraine, where the mere movement of your head produces vise-like pressure that doesn't subside. You can't tolerate noise. Even a whisper is like a shout. Light, even viewed from behind closed eyelids, is agony.

Imagine living with this and ask yourself: Would I want two friends sitting on either side of my bed, rubbing my arms back and forth, up and down, while talking incessantly? Don't think so. Would you want someone running their fingers through your hair or stroking your head? The very head you've been imagining drilling holes into to relieve the pressure? Would you enjoy someone spooning you when every joint, down to the last knuckle of your pinkie finger has your undivided attention? Would this be comforting to you, even from someone you love more than anyone else in the world?

No!

We've seen a dying person try to tolerate the intrusion of a loved one in what is often a single bed – crowded at the best of times. Even if they make no sound or movement, the face of the dying tells the story. The addition of another body next to the actively dying is a burden not a comfort. Caregivers often see the person's physical symptoms worsen when, with the most loving intentions, people insist on being in close physical contact. So however tempted you might be to climb into the bed with a dying loved one, don't do it.

If you truly want to comfort your loved one, think what you *would* want during the worst flu/migraine/ (maybe hangover) of your life. You'd want your own space. No stroking, no rubbing, no patting, no hovering. A dying person's need for space has nothing to do with whether they love you or not. It has to do with where they are on their own journey.

Physically, the bodily systems – circulatory, respiratory and elimination – are shutting down. Emotionally, they are preparing to go. The actively dying usually keep their eyes closed. They are withdrawing bit by bit from life here. This is normal – and necessary for their leaving to be as peaceful as possible. The touching and rubbing maybe be your way of holding onto them, of remembering the last times you held Mom's hand or touched your husband or father or dear friend's face, but it's also clinging, a physical drag on them. It makes their leaving harder, not easier.

Linda, a hospice nurse, had spent several nights at the hospice center with her mother. She hadn't slept, showered or seen her children in several days. Finally, exhausted, she decided to go home.

"Are you going to be mad if I am not here when you get back?" her mother asked.
"No I won't," I told her tearfully. "I'll understand."
"It felt good to spend the night in my own bed," Linda says now. At six in the morning, the hospice center called.
"I really think this is it," the nurse on the phone said.
"Tell her I am coming," I replied. "I got there and I slipped my hand over hers, dragging my body and a chair behind me before settling in next to her bed. I felt a definite squeeze. She nodded her head, barely. I said, "I am here; it's okay to go." Within fifteen minutes her respirations got longer and longer apart. Seconds before her last breath she squeezed my hand then pushed it away and drew back her hand. She had a smile and looked so peaceful, and her head tilted up. Then I watched her spirit leave her body. I watched her face go from having color and life to clay. The transformation was unbelievable.

"I immediately recalled an early teaching from one of the nuns at the hospice center. Never hold the hand of a dying person because you are holding them back. My mom had physically pushed my hand away, like, 'You have to let go. I have to go now.' I was filled with incredible peace."

So what *can* you do that will help ease both the loved one and yourself? Gently slide a hand *under* theirs, not on top. A hand on top feels like a restraint. A hand underneath says: *I support you; you are free to do what you need to do.* Play some of their favorite music, softly. Dim the lights. Light a candle. Talk – softly– about a road trip you took together, growing up together, the first time you met. Share something they did or said that had an impact on you. None of these things seem right for the person you've known? Then sit in silence.

TIP: Focus on being *with* them, not on what to do *to* them. To sit quietly with someone, letting them know you are there can be enough, and can be a great comfort to you both.

ANTICIPATORY GRIEF, AKA THE EEYORE SYNDROME

Some people experience anticipatory grief, i.e. mourning their loved one BEFORE the actual death, as did the sister of the AIDS patient in the hospice center. Some begin to grieve the day they learn of the terminal diagnosis, others when their loved one can no longer do the things they used to do, or when they can no longer get out of bed, or when it looks as though the end is near. The person experiencing anticipatory grief often begins to draw away from their dying loved one, absenting themselves from meaningful contact.

We call this The Eeyore Syndrome for A.A. Milne's perpetually negative character, Eeyore, in the Winnie the Pooh stories. Eeyore was the eternal pessimist, afraid to take joy in anything because he knew that at some point, the toy would be broken, the honey would be gone, the beautiful sunny day would eventually turn to rain. But mourning the loss before it's taken place – since we are all going to lose each other one day – cuts the anticipatory griever off from whatever pleasure they might share – or comfort they might offer – if they were to instead stay present in the moment. Sue and her colleagues have seen anticipatory grief lead to distancing oneself from the loved one – perhaps because the person wants to 'remember them as they were' or not intrude, or can't bear to see the loss of the person's abilities and health. It's understandable. Watching someone you care about slowly lose the things that had for much of their life given pleasure and meaning is just plain hard. And knowing that they will die soon is difficult (though sometimes after a long and painful journey toward death, there is legitimate relief – more about that later). But grieving the impending loss does not lessen the total aggregate amount of grief you will feel, as though you could pay down that debt earlier and therefore not experience an overwhelming balloon payment of grief at the actual death. Wanting to mitigate your pain at the death is completely understandable, but anticipatory grief often distances you from the person before they are gone. And with that, you are no longer available to comfort or to take comfort from their presence, and may be unable to receive whatever blessings or gifts, or comforting affirmations that may be on tap.

Jasper, who had AIDS, had spent several months at the hospice center, where his sister, Chloe visited every day. Her brother was wasting away; she knew he'd be gone soon. One day Maria, a hospice nurse, came in to give Jasper his medicine. He was in bed, dozing, but Chloe stood some distance away staring at him and crying. Maria had learned through years of experience, not to rush in to 'fix' people who were struggling with an impending death, so she simply sat down on the bed and gave Jasper the medicine. For a moment, she thought about getting up and leaving without a word. But, seeing that Chloe was already standing at Jasper's grave in her imagination, feeling the pain she was certain she would feel, Maria instead stood up at the bedside and reached out her hand.

"Jasper is with you now," she said to Chloe, motioning her to come close. "Be with him now,"

With those words, Chloe's whole demeanor changed. She came across the room to take her sleeping brother by the hand.

"You can't take the pain away from the person who's grieving," Maria said later. "It's not your pain. But you can be a catalyst for comfort. It's a fine line, though. You can blow it either way by under-doing or overdoing."

TIP: Being present with the dying can help you to be much less focused on your own impending loss. Will you anticipate the death and be sad about it? Of course. But don't let that overshadow and ruin the actual time you have together.

THE PARADE

You as caregiver or central contact person have made a phone call to a family member explaining the changes you're seeing in the dying loved one. The news spreads like a viral video. There's a knock at the door, it's a relative you haven't seen in months. An hour goes by, another knock, another relative. Before you realize it, there are twenty people in your home or the hospice center, nursing home or wherever the dying loved one may be. There are small children, bored, climbing on furniture, screaming, running up and down the stairs, and crying for attention. Then comes the food – clattering dishes, lip smacking, and the gurgling of sucking air through a straw for that last drop of soda. The noise level continues to rise as conversations compete and everyone forgets why they are really here. This liveliness may be comforting to you or to others, who feel an obligation to come but who are uncomfortable with being near the dying, but the noise, the smells, the over-stimulation can be very stressful for a person whose declining body can't find the physical strength or voice to shout: Please stop!

Go back to your worse flu/migraine/hangover and imagine how comforting you'd find a party in your bedroom. Not much. Yet with flu/migraine/hangover, you know (or assume) you'll recover and be up and among your friends and family again. This is different. This is coming down to the finish line, and everyone knows it. As a result, people want to come, be present and see the person for the last time. A nice sentiment. And for some, without all the hub-bub, a steady stream of friends coming to say goodbye can be a great solace, a sweet goodbye.

But a crush of people is not only not helpful, it's unfair to the dying person, who often feels they *should* try to participate in conversation and struggles to stay alert because you took the time to visit, or because they haven't seen you in a long time. It's exhausting, a major draw on their ebbing reserves of energy. Too many in one day pretty much guarantees the person will be withdrawn the next, and may even hasten the end.

This is not the same as the gentle flow of visitors that one friend received in his last days. He was at home, comfortable but declining fast, yet his friends and family came in quietly, sat with him, spoke with him for a little while as a way to say 'Goodbye, it's been so good to know you,' and left without fanfare. His widow later wrote to friends to thank them for the great pleasure it had given her husband to say goodbye to everyone who came.

CAREGIVER TIP: Keep the environment calm and peaceful. It's perfectly OK for a caregiver or patient advocate to limit the number of visitors. It's also OK to limit the amount of time a visitor can stay if necessary. Reassure the dying person it's okay to sleep even in the presence of visitors. (Nancy took a book to sit at the bedside of one friend seven days before he died while his wife went to church. Bob talked when he wanted to, and slept when he needed to until his wife returned, peaceful companionship to them both.). If you've called in hospice staff and feel unable to set boundaries with visitors, the staff will be able to be 'the bad guys' in this situation and limit the number of visitors and length of stay.

The caregiver has taken on a role that can be challenging; it's made more difficult when there is not complete cooperation from other family members and friends. Trying to navigate through a lifetime of family dysfunction is like shooting white water rapids in a rudderless raft. It's not the caregiver's job to entertain visitors, and, as noted, it can be extremely tiring for the dying person.

VISITOR TIP: Call first to find out if the person wants visitors. Some people will not, wanting to save their remaining energy for a very few family members or even a single friend or loved one. Some will not wish to be seen by others under these circumstances. Some dying people don't want to actually tell people not to come, but don't want them and so bottle up anger, resentment, and frustration at being burdened with these emotions at a time like this. If the caregiver says the person would welcome a visit, make it short. And be respectful of the caregiver's wishes.

Nancy went to see Bill, her friend and minister in the hospital during his last few days. He was ninety, had suffered a major stroke, and could hardly speak, but was obviously glad to see her. She stayed barely just long enough to tell him she loved him, give him a kiss, and as she leaned down to say goodbye, repeated the cheerful words he had always said to her when they parted after spending time together: "Until the next time!"

At that, he closed his eyes with a smile on his face, and she knew it was time to go. The visit, which meant much to her – and possibly to him, though she may never know – lasted about three minutes.

CAREGIVER TIP: Again, watch the face. Notice any changes in expression and in breathing patterns to indicate what the person is feeling. If things are going downhill, you can point that out to the visitor and gently suggest they come back another time.

The 'parade' may include some relative, friend or neighbor, who has been absent during the progression of the illness, who also thinks he or she should help decide how things are done – and lets everyone know it. This can be very stressful for both the actual decision-maker and for the dying loved one. Stress like this often has a physical impact on the dying person, exacerbating pain and/or shortness of breath.

That said, it helps to remember that even the second-guesser generally comes with good intentions. Letting go completely of another person is a time of high emotions that get expressed in a variety of ways – some of which can be incredibly obtuse, frustrating or pain-in-the-neck to the person on whose shoulders most of the care falls.

Anna Bowers observed in an essay she wrote in her blog: SaucedinNewYork, when her beloved grandmother died: "How we mourn is deeply personal, and while we often want to see our grief reflected back to us in a similar manner, we must accept that while some of us cry, others need to make jokes or appear stoic or keep busy. None are right. None are wrong. They simply are how we mourn."

CAREGIVER TIP: A good way to defuse the take-charge second-guesser is to acknowledge that everyone has his or her own relationship with the dying loved one. Allow each one five minutes alone with the dying person to say goodbye without an audience. This will not only empower the visitor, but may well help subdue disruptive attitudes, calm aggressive behavior, (which can be contagious), and get the focus back on what will help or comfort the dying loved one.

CAREGIVER TIP: If the second-guesser is still insistent that you must continue feeding, should not give too much painkiller, give more water, less water, a caregiver can say to the person: 'It must be easier to focus on [food, medicine, whatever] than to focus on the progression of the condition/disease and the fact that death is coming.' This can help people start to acknowledge (without the accompanying guilt for thinking it) that this is what impending death looks like.

Another possibility is: "This must be really hard for you," which could help them to realize that they need to focus on what really matters most during this last time with the person.

In addition to the emotional upheaval that may be running like a river through everyone concerned, it's unsettling to be around a dying person, particularly if it's the first time you have experienced a transition like this. There may be unpleasant odors. There may be bags hanging from the bed collecting bodily fluids, which can be even more disturbing to some than watching Dr. Oz hold up various organs on television. Often the person looks quite different from they way they did in health. They may be slack-jawed and breathing through the mouth. For those at the bedside, it may feel uncomfortable – disrespectful even – to just stare at them, yet it doesn't feel right to look away.

TIP: A photograph or two in the room from various stages of the person's life can be comforting reminders of happy times.

None of this means the dying person should be cut off from others (unless they want to be). There is a difference between a meaningful visit with the dying loved one and putting in an appearance. Time together is visibly ebbing, so make sure that the time spent with that person is time spent well.

When Nancy's father-in-law, who doted on his grandchildren, was in the hospital for the last time, she and her husband took their two children, then nine and eleven, to see him. Though he was within days of dying of cancer and was exhausted with the physical toll it was taking, he was alert and was especially pleased to see his son and the children. They sat in chairs at the foot of his bed where he could easily see them all. He asked the children about what they were doing, listened with obvious pleasure and attention not only to what they were saying, but to who they were, what kind of legacy he was leaving behind.

The family stayed 20 minutes. They took their cue to exit when the light went out in his face, he sank down quietly, turned over on his side, and started to dose off. Before leaving, each of the family went to him, kissed him goodbye, and whispered that they loved him.

On the way home, nine-year-old Abby observed, "He was drinking us in."

He died, peacefully, two days later. The visit was a final gift that he gave to his grandchildren and they to him.

CAREGIVER AND VISITOR TIP: Consider who the person was during in their active life, and proceed accordingly.

THE SHIFT

The Shift refers to the restlessness often exhibited by the dying. It can last minutes to hours – usually not more than a day, though there is no set pattern. This too, can come and go days or even weeks before death, though it more often happens when the person is quite close to leaving. This restlessness can take several forms:

- The person may make repetitive motions such as picking at clothing, at sheets or at the air.
- They may make repetitive actions like trying to get out of bed. They may insist you help them out of bed, and then seconds later demand to get back in, repeating this sequence over and over.
- They may talk about taking a trip and the need to get ready, may even talk about packing for it or getting train or plane tickets. They may insist you come with them.
- They may blurt out they are dying.
- They may seem confused and disoriented about where they are or who you are
- They may ask a series of questions. Where am I? What's going on here? Why am I here? Who are you? Who am I?
- They may be incredibly irritable or anxious or suddenly lash out at family and friends, making irrational accusations. This is tough to watch, let alone try to respond to, but bear in mind, this is not about you. This is *their* reality.

FIRST, BREATHE

CAREGIVER TIP: Safety of the person is the first priority. Do not try to interfere, which can exacerbate the person's agitation; simply protect them from injury. Rule out pain, a full bladder, constipation, or respiratory distress as a possible cause. If the potential physical symptoms have been eliminated, and the restlessness and /or agitation persist, consider spiritual distress.

VISITOR and CAREGIVER TIP: Gently remind them of who they are, where they are, and what they mean to you. If they have been actively religious, have the minister, rabbi or other spiritual mentor make a visit. In a calm and soothing manner, remind them of their faith, recite prayers with them if that has been their habit and history. If they have no formal religiosity, simply speak gently to them about who and where they are, reassure them that they are being cared for and are not alone. This may or may not work. Even if none of this works, it's not your fault.

This disoriented agitation may be disturbing to you as observer, because you want to comfort and calm the person; not being able to makes you feel helpless. (Let's face it: for the most part, you are helpless.). This restlessness is often a sign that the person has suddenly felt a shift: something's different; something's changed. Instinctively the person feels they are close to dying – no one needs to tell them this, they feel it. It's a big transition; hence, the restlessness. They may feel restless because it's out of their control. Perhaps because they have unfinished business and there is no time to tend to it. Or perhaps because they are worried about making life's biggest transition.

Sedation might seem like a quick fix and in some circumstances it's necessary and the best thing for them. But suppose these are their last moments of alertness? Ask yourself: Would I want awareness of this last time here to be medicated away if it were me? Do I want it for the person I love? There can be surprising – and precious – moments of lucidity just when you think there will be none any more.

Nancy's father, bedridden with cancer, had been through the restlessness for several days prior to his death, distracted and not sure where he was. He calmed in the last couple of days, but had still not known her when she arrived to sit with him one day. Yet the following day, he suddenly opened his eyes, grabbed her by the arm, called her by name and told her he loved her. He died the following day. The reassurance this last word of love her father spoke to her – and its urgency – helped ease the pain of the parting.

CAREGIVER AND VISITOR TIP: Remain calm. Reassure the person with soft music, aromatherapy, memories of their favorite people, places or experiences. Let them know that you will be okay, that everyone they are leaving behind will miss them but will be fine, that you will tend to those they may worry about and that it's okay to let go of that responsibility. Generally, once a person gets past the restlessness, they fall into a deep peaceful coma-like place and don't come back.

TIP: If reassuring the person doesn't help and the anxiety continues, medication is appropriate.

During the last few hours of Nancy's father's life her stepmother was certain that, while he, a gifted musician, could not respond, he could hear music. She continually put classical records on, which seemed to soothe him, and he breathed his last to the strains of Mozart's 40th symphony.

Another friend, a poet and harpist, played the harp for her husband while he was dying.

"I could tell it helped him," she said. Eleven years later, she is in a program to provide music for those in hospice care.

THE SMILE

If you are lucky, you may see what some hospice workers call *The Smile*. This smile, different from those in everyday life, is utterly blissful; it illuminates the dying person's face with a look of absolute peace. For those watching, it offers a sense of incredible comfort, reassurance that for the dying all is well; all is OK.

Most of the time, this smile appears very shortly before death. One such smile is the one that Sue witnessed on the face of Robert, a man in his forties. He had walked into the hospice center only days before, but was now stretched out in bed virtually immobile with his head propped on several pillows. His face, which had once had a warm Mediterranean glow, was now pasty grey. Dark circles accentuated hollowed eyes, and mouth breathing heightened the gaunt appearance. He had no strength to even open his eyes. The hospice staff had gathered the family several times with: "It won't be long; I think it will be today," a well-meaning alert that can turn into an emotional roller coaster for the family if, as in Robert's case, it turns out to be premature. After two weeks of this, the family asked the staff not to offer any more predictions. Late one afternoon, Robert's wife, Maria, sat in a folding chair next to the bed, bent over and resting her head on her folded arms by his hip. Her eyes were closed. Sue, who had stayed close to Maria ever since Robert's arrival in the center, stood behind her.

Then it happened.

"The sun was hidden behind clouds and the light hadn't changed," Sue remembers, "but his face sure did."

Robert's ashen color noticeably brightened. Though his eyes were still closed, a smile very slowly began to take shape. Sue, her eyes on Robert's face, tapped Maria on the shoulder. She lifted up her head and stared at her husband.

"There's the smile I told you about," Sue whispered in Maria's ear.

The smile grew, exposing teeth and gums as if he might actually laugh. His face appeared to be surrounded by a white brilliance. A minute, maybe two passed, then, with a confused look, he opened his eyes, and turned his head toward Maria.

"Robert, where have you been?" she asked.

Their eyes met for an instant; a different smile came over his face, a more down-to-earth smile, as the illumination faded and his color returned to a deathly pallor. He closed his eyes again without answering.

"That smile gave me an amazing sense of peace and well-being," Maria said later.

"After the smile I had no more worries ever about my husband's fate. I realized how much I had been trying (even determined) to control his inner experience. But his inner experience was his own, always was, and he was doing just fine with it. At that realization I could let go."

While this blissful, illuminated smile can appear toward the very end of a life, it has, on rare occasions, appeared on a person's face after clinical death. Eerie perhaps, but also amazing, since smiling uses muscles that go slack in death, which makes that smile not only astonishing (and kinda spooky), but also encouraging.

Sue, who for years had listened to her colleagues talk about the post-mortem smile, had never seen it before. Until Lois.

Lois was a young-looking 65-year-old dying of cancer. She was in great pain – her belly hugely bloated and, despite periodic draining, continually filling with fluid. There were measures the hospice nurses were taking to help alleviate Lois's distress, but it was clear that her time was coming to an end. Sue had met Lois on Friday; she saw the yellow color of Lois's eyes – a sign of liver failure. When she returned to her shift the following day, Sue could see by the physical changes in Lois's color that she had clearly taken a big step. This was IT. And soon. To prepare the family for what was imminent, Sue invited the family – husband, Tim, son, Cory, and daughter, Jody, into the hallway.

"I tried to warn them gently, about what they could expect, about what changes were forthcoming," Sue says. "The men glared at me, but Jody softened and pulled out her camera, showing me pictures of her mother that she had taken in the hospital the previous week."

In every shot there was a brilliant white ball of light by the left side of Lois's head. Jody had taken pictures of everyone else while standing next to Lois, but none had that light. It only showed up when Lois was alone in the shot.

"The nurse at the hospital told me that was her guardian angel," Jody said.

"They were not a religious family in the traditional sense," Sue remembers, "but Jody's story seemed to comfort Tim and Cody."

The family had stayed the night with Lois; all were exhausted. They decided to go home to rest, leaving Cody's wife, Shirley, with Lois.

"You'll call us if anything changes, won't you?" Jody asked.

"Of course."

Sue watched the three of them trudge down the hall, then stepped into Lois's room to check on her. Afternoon sun poured through the open French door filling the room with buttery light. Outside the gardens were blooming with the colors and textures of an impressionist painting. Lois was lying on her back with the head of the bed slightly elevated, apparently asleep, her beauty shining through despite her faded, sallow complexion. Although Lois did not react to voices, Shirley insisted she was responding to them.

There had been no apparent change in Lois for about three hours when Shirley called for a nurse. Sue responded. Lois had lost her yellow color; she was pale gray. Sue called the family then went to check on another patient. By the time she got back to Lois's room, Jody was sitting on the side of the bed crying, talking to her mother, rubbing her forearm. Lois was taking only three breaths a minute with 20-second lapses in between. Tim and Cory crashed through the French doors just in time to see Lois take her last breath. Sue put a stethoscope to Lois's chest for two minutes and listened. Nothing. Finally, she turned to the family.

"It's over. Her suffering is over."

Sue then stepped out of the room, leaving the family to grieve in private. About 45 minutes later, she went back in. Tim was sitting on a chair on one side of the bed with Cory standing behind him alongside Shirley. Jody was sitting on a chair on the other side of the bed.

Sue commented to Jody how beautiful Lois looked even in death.

Then it happened.

The corners of Lois's mouth pulled up into a smile. There seemed to be a radiant glow around her. Jody saw it.

"Would it be too weird if I took a picture?" she asked.

"Please do! You need to document this!" Sue replied.

This extraordinary moment, this smile, was something Sue had heard about from other hospice nurses for years, but until then had never witnessed. She wanted to shout for joy, leap and run down the hall, telling everyone. Instead, she said to the family:

"She is letting you know that all is well. What a wonderful gift. You hold onto that."

That Smile was a gift to Sue as well — and to all hospice caregivers who daily minister to the dying and their grieving loved ones — a sign that this is not IT. The Smile offers hope that there is more to come.

Chapter Eleven

PEACE IN THE STILLNESS

Hospice workers use words like 'privilege,' 'honor' and 'blessing' when discussing being present at the time of death. What exactly does that mean? For Sue, it means the feeling of peace in the stillness of the deceased. It is palpable. There is an instant calmness. The face relaxes, the body relaxes and there is stillness in their heart. It is a bittersweet pivotal moment in time. Time stands still.

Chapter Twelve

AFTERMATH: THE FIRST MONTHS

"Being there with him at that moment made me not afraid of death," said Anne. "I could tell he was fine. And that helped me a lot."

BREATHE

However you and the people closest to you mark this moment of finality —
a last kiss or touch, a toast, a prayer, or with something more dramatic
(Nancy's stepmother flung herself across the body, wailing, while the
daughter of a friend immediately began texting everyone she knew), or with
quiet thanks for the life you shared with this person — this is a watershed
time in your life. Even when we think we are prepared for it, the moment
when life leaves the body is a shock. You may feel stunned that what you
knew was coming, that what you may even have hoped for or prayed for at
times, but thought would never come, is actually here. That's it. You may
feel sadness, wrenching loss, relief, guilt, overwhelming love, abandonment
or you may feel all of them and more in a carousel of emotions. Or you
may feel numb.

*For Nancy's mother-in-law, it had been a long, slow, but relatively painless decline.
During the last weeks and final days, the family had come in rotation and occasionally
gathered together, sat by the hospital bed that had been installed in the home, held her
hand, and said their goodbyes. None should have been surprised when she breathed her
last and her heart stopped.*

And yet….

"She's gone," Gary said, looking across the fields.

*They were walking the dogs on a beautiful summer morning. He had stopped to
answer his phone, listened for a few moments then put the cell back in his pocket. He
looked shell-shocked.*

"Are you OK?"

"Yeah," he said.

"How do you feel?" Nancy asked as they turned toward home.

*Gary stopped walking, paused and thought for a long moment, then replied:
"Disconnected."*

That sense of disconnection may come and go over the next few days
during what is often a flurry of activity as the most immediate decisions
about the disposition of the body, who's in charge (sometimes a disputed
category), what things take priority and how they will be dealt with are
made. Unless the person either wrote down or told those who will be in a

position to implement his or her wishes for a funeral or ceremony, there could be disputes. Many people feel very strongly about ceremony, what kind of rite or ritual should mark the passing and honor the person. Often these strong feelings are voiced strongly, too, regardless of whether the person voicing them has the authority to decide. One thing to remember: the funeral or memorial of whatever description is meant to honor the person who is gone, but it is also meant to comfort those who remain behind. It's not designed to prove to your bossy sibling once and for all who Mom loved best, or prove by its lavishness or drama how important everyone involved is. It's not designed to *prove* anything to anyone. It's meant to comfort the grieving and say goodbye to the deceased. Period.

DON'T STAND ON CEREMONY

It also bears remembering that there are many different comforting – even uplifting – ways to say goodbye to a loved one. Gary's mother had not attended church and had left no instructions for a funeral, memorial or any kind of ritual following her death. She had opted in writing for cremation, but left what followed, if anything, to her three children to decide. Fortunately, there was discussion among them, but not dispute. Acknowledging their mother's non-affiliation with institutions or formal religion, they initially thought they would do nothing. But after a day's thought, they decided that a simple memorial gathering in the house she had loved would not only be appropriate to the person she was, but would be a heartening way for them to mark the passage. They also knew it would comfort them to have people there who had meant something to their mother and for whom she had meant something. They invited a few friends, the daughters-in-law brought food, and following a brief homily by the hospice chaplain, all shared reminiscences of the woman who had been such a fixture in their lives. She had been an excellent cook who enjoyed a party and loved beautiful things, which made the gathering a fitting tribute and goodbye for those who loved her most.

Others choose other ways to mark a loved one's passing. Following the memorial service for his father, one grown son put some of the ashes (cremains) in several baby food jars, and over the course of a year, quietly sprinkled them in a few of his father's favorite places. In a different approach to ceremony, a bereaved sister quietly buried her troubled brother's casket next to their father's without mourners at the graveside. Then, in an effort to give him a send-off she knew her brother would have appreciated, she held a memorial party for him at a sports bar – beer, loud music, plenty of tailgate party food. A stack of his T-shirts sat beside a corkboard filled with pictures of him throughout his life. His sister urged his many friends to each take a T-shirt (there were dozens). Some were emblazoned with his favorite sports teams, some with beach logos, others with sayings that reminded the wearers of their late buddy. And after a beery-loud celebration of Andrew's life, each left with a little piece of his wardrobe as a tangible remembrance of him.

Two days after the death of Sue's father, a package arrived at his house. It contained a man's suit, white shirt, leather shoes and three ties, one red, one orange and one yellow.

"Dad's funeral clothes, I thought," Sue says now. "Dad hadn't worn leather shoes for years after his toe was amputated, which was just more confirmation to me that he knew his time was limited."

Then Sue saw the three new ties – loud, wildly patterned – like all the others that had always been his trademark.

"I wondered why three ties, but maybe he thought he'd have the time to select one to be laid out in. Or maybe he though there'd be one for each of his two sons and his son-in-law. We'll never know," Sue says. "But I thought immediately, "Wouldn't it be nice if each of them wore a 'Paul tie' to the funeral?"

Then she thought – why stop with three?

"I went to his closet," she says. "There were Mickey Mouse ties, (Micky and Dad shared the same birthday), skinny ties from the 60's, wide ties from the 70's – all the decades represented in a unique and fun fashion. I put them in a bag and then brought them to the church for the pallbearers to select a 'Paul tie' to wear."

"As people began to file into the church, I held the bag of 'Paul ties' bursting with color and pattern," Sue remembers, "and I felt as though my father's personality seemed to come alive. Friends and family recognized the ties the pallbearers were wearing. First one neighbor asked, "Can I wear a Paul tie?" He reached into the bag of ties with the excitement of a child on Christmas morning, replaced his tie, lifted his head and smiled. Another asked, then another, until several men and one woman were proudly wearing a 'Paul.'"

"Watching folks tie one on changed my glum mood, and I had the feeling my father was smiling down on them," Sue says now. "It's a gesture that friends and family still bring up at funerals."

Funerals, memorial services and other rituals, which can be as varied as the people and relationships involved, mark a coda in that life and that time. These rituals also offer a time during which we gather to acknowledge what that person's life meant in the community of friends and family. Many people dread funerals, but they can be surprisingly uplifting to those closest to the person who is gone. Looking around at the other faces and seeing that you are not alone in mourning helps.

THE REST IS SILENCE – FOR A WHILE

If there is a service of some kind following the death, there will be an intense few days, then silence. For the primary caregiver, who has been living every day with this impending death, after weeks or months of loved-one-focused days, there's silence. You may find yourself walking into a room to tell them something, and there's silence. This adds to a sense of disconnectedness.

"You expect to feel a sense of relief when someone is gravely ill and you don't want them to suffer any more," says Stephanie. "But you really feel completely unmoored. This thing that was chaining you was also what was anchoring you. I first remember not knowing where I was going. And it was very distressing. There's this giant hole where the care of this person used to be. Also, the illness set all your priorities, which in some ways made life easier – talk about don't sweat the small stuff! The little stuff doesn't even arise to the level of notice, so in a way life becomes very streamlined and simpler. [Then when they die] you really feel adrift and isolated. [Also] I was fairly young when I was widowed [44], so I didn't have a lot of friends who'd been through this."

You may find yourself at the grocery store cruising up and down the aisles in a fog, barely aware of the voices and people; you can't remember what you came for. You're running on autopilot. You feel disorganized; you may question who you are, whether life makes sense any more, and whether it can ever make sense again. This is grief.

Janet spotted a former colleague at the grocery store. Usually meticulous, the woman looked as though she had slept in her clothes. Janet came up to her and asked how she was doing.
"I just lost my husband," she told Janet. "I don't know who I am!"

Loosing a life partner may feel as though part of you is missing, not unlike the phantom pain people can feel after an amputation. You may go back to relive the moment of death often in the following weeks and months. Sadness, loss of appetite, struggling to maintain focus are signs of depression, but they're also signs of grieving. This is normal. Stephanie, who is a writer, describes feeling numb for months following her husband's death.

"You're really in shock," she says. "I had no ability to focus. I couldn't even read a book, which is terrible for me – you're not capable of that kind of sustained focus; it's like brain fog. That hangs in for a good long while. My husband died in September and I never wrote a word while he was sick [and for several months afterward] even though I'd been working on poetry before he was diagnosed. He was so much my focus I couldn't get outside of it enough to write about it."

During these first months, you may feel perpetually on edge, off-balance and irritated with everything and everyone. You may crave companionship and still not be able to tolerate actual people. You're not crazy, though it may feel like it at times. This is normal. Friends may want to help – and they *can* simply by being there.

"I didn't know what to say to people," says Stephanie. "You want to tell people there's nothing you can say that is the right thing, but nothing that is the wrong thing, either. It's just making contact. You just need to know people are reaching out. The fact of the offer is somehow comforting."

PAUSE

TIP: Give yourself time to adjust. Talking periodically with a friend, a therapist, religious leader or other mentor can help. Make a date with a friend for coffee or lunch when you're feeling desperately sad or alone.

TIP: If you don't want to see people for a little while, when someone shows up at your doorstep because they haven't heard from you in days and are worried about you, it's okay to say something like: " I really appreciate your support and stopping by, but I am very tired and just need to lie down. Let's schedule another time."

But remember that we are social beings. Even the most reticent and private of souls needs human contact. It helps.

Some people who rushed in to help toward the end may stick around for a few weeks immediately following the death then become unavailable not long afterward. Perhaps they have done their part for now and need to go back to their own routines – everyone has his or her own set of problems and worries in addition to helping you through this. Some friends may fall silent not long after the death for fear of reminding you of your loss (as though you could forget), or for fear of saying the wrong thing. They may be afraid of your tears, the enormity of your grief. People may find it difficult to gauge when you want to be alone (indeed, you may find it difficult to gauge when you want to be alone) and don't want to intrude. They may think you need this time alone. You *may* need it – to catch up on paperwork, stand in the shower and sob until you can't any more, look through old pictures, or deal with the mundane but often deadline-ridden details immediately following a death. You may find it difficult to muster the energy to be with people, who are not dealing with what you are dealing with right now. You may find it stressful to be with people whose lives seem to be perfect while yours feels like it's falling apart.

TIP: Consciously develop a new routine. Phone a friend during the time you were usually making dinner or doing something for the deceased. Go to the farmers' market on Saturday morning just to be with people and to see life and liveliness. Stop at the library on the way home from work, stop into the same café each afternoon for a cup of tea – they'll get to know you and you can get to know them, but they won't require anything of you save for paying the check (and maybe a tip). Connect with people who can offer a little conversation, a few comforting words, a little understanding or simply their caring presence if you don't feel like talking. Read some poetry written by someone who's been through what you're going through. Go to a movie, garden (seeing the cycle of life in the earth can offer perspective) or take a walk – fresh air and sunshine are clinically healing.

Some people may probe for details of the death, a very private matter unless you start the conversation. You may want to hear about what a friend went through when her mother died, or it may make you want to run away screaming.

TIP: If you don't feel like talking about it, say so – "I'm not ready to go over it, I don't feel like talking right now, I'm simply not up to this conversation" – there are several ways to ask people to back off without taking their heads off. If the question brings you to tears, unless they're completely obtuse, they'll probably change the subject immediately – or offer a hug, which may help. Take care of yourself without alienating those who are probably trying to comfort you.

In that vein, you may be on the receiving end of a string of platitudes:

> It was his time.
> She's at peace now.
> At least she's no longer suffering.
> It's probably a blessing.
> Keep yourself busy.
> Time heals all wounds.
> God needed another angel.
> Things will be back to normal soon; you wait and see.
> Or the mother of all statements never to say to either the dying or the
> bereaved: I know how you feel. (Regardless of whether that's true).

These road-worn bromides may comfort you, or they may make you feel like slapping the person. Whichever your response, try to bear in mind that their words are simply evidence that people feel helpless and are just trying to say: "I'm sorry for your loss." They want you to feel better (you want to feel better too, but it's going to be an up and down process that will take time). Go easy on them and on yourself.

REWINDING AND REPLAYING: WOULDA SHOULDA COULDA

You jolt awake at 3a.m., haunted by what you did for the deceased during those last weeks and days, by what you think you woulda done had you known more, what you coulda done and didn't, and by what you shoulda done differently. You begin to question every little decision, every task performed. The inner critic may start up: "I could have done better!" "What makes you think you knew what you were doing?" "Maybe I should have called in more professionals even if I couldn't afford it!" " You're not trained!" " What if, what if, what if?" You may worry what family and friends think about the care you offered.

Allowed to continue unchecked the inner critic can promote headaches, nausea, bingeing, diarrhea, or sleepless nights. Not helpful. It can be tempting to numb the critic with alcohol, or maybe leftover painkillers (a dangerous venture), but these things are depressants. You're grieving, which is depressing; you don't need to be chemically depressed, too. And just as important, it won't silence the shoulda's coulda's. Calm, reasonable assessment can. And never underestimate the benefits of fresh air – a walk in the sunshine promotes endorphins, which can help calm you, and can become a therapeutic ritual in itself.

BREATHE

Instead of replaying a list of imagined (or even real) shortcomings in the care you gave your loved one, consciously rewind and then play the mental tape of what you did for them. Look back through your journal if you kept one. Find something reassuring that will remind you what you did to make their day better – shared a meaningful conversation or a quiet moment of handholding, talked over your life together, watched a film that you both enjoyed, made sure to put flowers where she could see them easily, was there to reassure him when he most needed your presence. Reminisce with a family member or friend who shared a visit with the deceased. Focus only on the good by writing or talking with those involved in the care to validate all you accomplished. This will help affirm the compassionate, loving – and challenging – role you played in this process and will help to silence the inner critic.

You did the best you could with the knowledge, energy, and resources you had at the time. You can't change what's happened, so try to let it go. Chastising yourself for imagined shortcomings is only useful if it helps you learn something. Otherwise, it's not only unproductive, it's downright damaging to your health.

List how you fulfilled your loved one's wishes and needs. For example:

> He/she got a good night sleep because I called the doctor and got some medicine.
> I brought in some oxygen and it eased her breathing.
> I prepared a favorite dish and he enjoyed it.
> I was able to take her to a cherished place.
> I ordered his favorite movie to watch and share some laughs.
> I was able to bring some dear friends to visit.
> I read aloud from her favorite book or magazine until she fell asleep.
> We spent a day reminiscing about …..
> _____ was the hardest thing I had to do, but he needed it, so I did it anyway.
> Jot down a special memory of that time that will encourage you going forward and stick it someplace – like your desk drawer – that you will come across regularly.

TIP: Grief is exhausting! Recharge your body with rest, exercise, nourishment and the kindness of others.

After three months, people may encourage you to move on. They may suggest you clear out your loved one's belongings. You may be ready to do that in the first three weeks, or not for the first six or eight months (or years). When her mother died, Nancy's father couldn't bear to touch his wife's clothes, but he wanted her closet cleared that week, so Nancy did it. She saved a few of the things that she had most loved to see her mother wear and stuck them in her own closet, then gave some of her mother's clothes to friends; seeing her mother's beautiful things being enjoyed by others was comforting for Nancy particularly as she knew her stylish but frugal mother would have approved. When her father died, she helped her brother clear out their father's closet and took home one of his sweaters; she wore it without washing it for two years because it still smelled of her dad. Some people insist that having a picture of the person on the pillow or wearing his favorite scarf every day for weeks is just plain nuts. It's not. We all have different timetables for grief

THERE MIGHT BE DRAGONS

People react to the death of a loved one in wide range of ways, but as with a terminal diagnosis, it's often personality times ten among those the person leaves behind, at least for a while. Often, it's not a pretty sight. Dragons emerge breathing fire or spewing venom or other unpleasantness at the most unexpected things. It may have started before the death, or it can start immediately afterward, focused first on the ceremony that follows. This can blindside you – even if you knew this person was not all that easy to deal with at the best of times. And it's exhausting, at a time when you're already wrung out and running on your last nerve.

Moments after his father died at home, one man immediately took the wireless telephone from the charger (this was before the ubiquitous cell phone), put it in his pocket and insisted that his sister and stepmother apply to him if they wanted to make a phone call.

In another case, when her grandmother died, a granddaughter went through all the drawers in the house looking for pictures to be sure she had them all in her possession 'for safekeeping.'

A stepmother, who had tried to give away the dog her husband and his daughter had shared, immediately laid claim to the dog following her husband's death. When the dog wandered down to the stepdaughter's nearby home, the stepmother threatened to sue the young woman for alienation of the dog's affections.

Following the funeral service that he did not attend for his brother, an uncle phoned his grieving, twenty-something niece from France to chew her out for what he perceived as her shortcomings in her father's end of life care.

When her father died, another woman was stunned to hear: "Dad always liked me best, so he'd want me to have more," from the brother she thought she knew and was always really close to.

In still another family, a cousin, who had been named an executor of his aunt's will, harshly told the three grieving children, who had gathered to choose a single personal memento following their mother's funeral: "No one touches anything!"

This kind of graceless behavior immediately following the death of a loved one can knock you flat. You thought you knew these people. Yes, maybe you'd had your differences, but you never expected this from them, not right now. You thought they might step up and offer support, kindness, and generosity of spirit, a kind of emotional group-hug-among-the-grieving; instead they make demands, offer criticism, want a bigger piece of the 'pie' or all of the above.

Among some, the blame game begins: The primary caregiver should have been more vigilant, tried a new therapy, taken the person out more, kept him or her at home longer, brought in more visitors, fewer visitors, loved them more, given them more medicine, food, care, less medicine, food, care, not called in hospice so soon, or so late. In short, done it all SO differently. These accusations often come from those who had little or no hands-on contact with the day-to-day caregiving. It can be a shock, particularly since you may already have a continuous guilt loop playing in your head for your own perceived or imagined shortcomings.

Some people want to claim *things* immediately following a loved one's death. In one case, an artist's grieving widow was barraged with calls and emails pestering her for keepsakes of her late husband's life. In another, a stepmother hid her stepdaughter's family silver to claim it as her own. In still another when a grown son died after a protracted battle with cancer, the young man's father came in one day when no one was around and walked off with an original watercolor that his ex-wife, the young man's mother had given her son on his last birthday. Whether this thing-grab stems from a desire to hold onto a memento that will remind these people of a special moment or be visible proof of the relationship they shared with the departed or from greed, or from a desire to somehow monopolize the person and the memories connected with them, or from fear of losing out to other greedy relatives, or from a sense of trying to control something – anything – is probably best left to the psychologists. If you experience this, complain to understanding friends over a beer or something, and try to do the right thing, but don't try to fix your dysfunctional family – find your own support, and let them find theirs.

If you as primary caregiver are also the primary one left to sort out the practical details that follow a death as well as knit together the pieces of your life after this intense journey, you already have enough on your plate. You're not obliged to respond to every demand, every accusation or need, every email or note or phone call if it does not legitimately bear on the nuts and bolts of taking care of the business immediately in front of you. (In terms of paperwork and such, the first six months are usually the most chore-filled). Sometimes, as mentioned in Chapter 10, How to Sit with The Actively Dying, a kind word 'turneth away wrath' and will defuse things when one of the dragons starts breathing fire down your neck. Despite the fact that you may really want to whomp 'em one, not rising to the bait of someone who is in-your-face complaining, demanding, even threatening is usually the better course in the long run. A gentle "back off" could do the trick (which can also be articulated as "I'm sorry, I can't cope with this right now." (Also, dropping your voice rather than raising it often helps to defuse emotional people.). You can't un-say harsh words to someone you may still love regardless of their shortcomings, their churlish behavior or your past disagreements. Maybe they'll remember those hurtful words, and it will blight your relationship going forward (though you may not care). In any case, it's worth choosing your words if you can, while being firm with the dragons.

Many women particularly have a hard time saying no to even the most ridiculous and unfounded demands that people make. But being able – or learning – to say no at this time is critical to taking care of yourself. If you find that you are either incapable of saying 'No' in one form or another ("I'm sorry, I can't," "My lawyer told me not to make any decisions without her," "My kids/siblings/mother/father/husband would kill me...") then disconnect from the person, at least for a while. Sue likes to disarm those who approach her with harsh words about how things should be done with a few calm words of her own: "This must be hard on you," she says, which sometimes stops people in their tracks. If they are at all perceptive, this can help them to think for a moment about what is coming out of their mouths – and perhaps out of their hearts. (We can all be pretty selfish and self-absorbed at times, but most of us don't actually want to be). If the person returns with a new approach, well and good. If not, try not to sweat it.

SIMULTANEOUSLY RAW, VULNERABLE AND NUMB

You are already raw; everything brings you to tears. You run across an article in the paper you want to share with the departed and for a split-second forget that he or she is gone until it hits you with a jolt. Your eye lights on something that reminds you of the person and you suddenly can't swallow past the lump in your throat. You pull a jacket out of the closet and are overwhelmed with the smell of them. You have a long list of things to take care of, yet you can't seem to figure out what to tackle first. One friend, who lost her husband when her sons were in their early teens, says she spent the first year walking around in what felt like a terminal fog. Even those who believe they are prepared for the death can find themselves in a kind of never-land immediately afterward.

Despite a slow and progressive lead-up to Nancy's mother-in-law's peaceful and expected death in her own home in her late 80's, her husband's response the morning of her death was shock.

"I feel disembodied," he told her as they drove the two hours to his mother's house

to gather with his siblings. "I don't know what I feel."

It had been anticipated, and was in some ways a relief, yet he still felt numb. The following week, while at the house, discussing the business of sorting out her things with his siblings, he put his hand on a 60-year-old copy of A.A.Milne's Now We Are Six *and broke down.*

"She used to read this to me," he explained tearfully.

Emotions are often raw at this time. Transitions of any kind – and this is a huge transition for everyone connected to the loved one – are rarely easy. People are often feeling their way through personally uncharted territory.

Having dragons around when you're feeling particularly vulnerable and possibly alone is no help. Worse, it can complicate things in a host of ways both material and emotional. It helps to have sensible steadfast friends you can bounce some of this stuff off of to calibrate your response. When his family wants to come take away the desk that your husband of ten years used because it had belonged to his mother – is it right that the childless widow keep it because it means so much to her? Or should she give it back because it means so much to the brother who asked for it? Like many things, it depends on the people and the situation. Calm, sensible, caring friends, who have no real skin in the game, can help to sort out the reasonable from the irrational and give you considered feedback. If you don't want to discuss the specifics of personal family business with friends, perhaps a minister, rabbi, or other trusted professional could help.

Psychiatrist Elizabeth Kubler-Ross articulated what she called the five stages of grief – denial, anger, bargaining, depression, and acceptance – in her groundbreaking book, *On Death and Dying*, which was inspired by her work with terminally ill patients in the 1960's. While this was dealing with those who were dying, rather than those they left behind, over the years, our bottom-line culture seems to have assimilated those stages as a kind of grief checklist, as though once you've experienced one stage on the list, you've graduated from that stage, and can go on to the next, eventually getting through all of it like some kind of advanced-level course. Grieving rarely works like that. It's more like a kaleidoscope, and it's hard to predict what you will be feeling at any given time, particularly initially. Most human beings who grieve will go through each of those stages at some point, though those emotional stages can come and go in no particular order.

Grief is messy (like much of life in our experience). People rarely feel just one thing at a time. We often feel a roiling stew of things simultaneously – things that can be completely at war with one another. Which brings us to relief and guilt.

When a loved one who had been suffering, whose care took an enormous amount of time, energy (both emotional and physical) and possibly money, dies after an arduous decline, relief is natural. But it's often a guilty secret that few caregivers will acknowledge. It probably shouldn't be. Relief is a legitimate response to the release, however much you loved the person, however conflicted or devoted the relationship, however much you will miss them, however much you may have resented the hurdles, shortcomings, frustrations, and the subsequent dragons you now must slay in the aftermath. Relief is not only an appropriate emotion; it may just enable you to move on, realistically, with the rest of your own life.

Nancy admits that the first thing she felt when her beloved father died was relief. "We all did our best, and gave him our best," she says now. "Whether it was 'enough' or not is not really a practical question. He had lived the way he wanted to. The last few months were very hard, and although our stepmother was his primary caregiver, my brother and I tag-teamed it, and one or the other of us went to see him and take care of things – and help our stepmother – every single day. My brother and I each had young children and were working. It was a 40-mile drive one way for me, and a 25-mile drive for my brother, so in addition to everything else in our lives, we were each on the road a lot. When he died, I knew I would miss him – I still do after all these years – but I was relieved not only that he wouldn't suffer any more, but that I would not have to do that any more."

However, losing a parent in adulthood, while sad, is part of the natural order. A parent has raised you and released you to your own life. No matter how close you have been, it is not the same thing as losing a spouse or life partner with whom you've shared breakfast or coffee virtually every day, supper together in the evening, sitting in front of the TV, going out to a movie or party, asked about where they put the car keys or why they never close any drawer they open or never pick up their own socks. Even if the days are routine, they are shared. Your lives were intertwined, the timing and logistics interwoven.

The relationship was an investment in time, energy, emotion and love. The person – their needs, their presence, their input – was a huge part of a life that you built together. You may even feel as though having a life partner is what gives you purpose in your own life. Additionally, you are missing the person with whom you made major decisions, perhaps worried together over children, friends or family, relied on for commiseration and emotional support, sacrificed to meet shared goals, planned how to pay bills, shared both public and private joys, sorrows, affection and secrets. The loss of that person is nearly palpable, something that can leave you seesawing between intense loneliness and anger at the fact that they have left. One friend lamented not long after her husband died: *"I'm glad he's not suffering any more, but I can't figure out why I'm still here. I just want to be with him. Why couldn't he take me too?"*

The loss of a child is a different kind of grief accompanied by an internal monologue that wails: How could I have changed that/protected him/done something differently so she would still be here?' coupled with all the imagined life milestones that will now never be shared and the piercing loss of a life's – and the next generation's – possibility.

Whoever you have lost, this is a very tough time. You are taking stock of where you are emotionally, spiritually, and financially. And the dragons may have something to say – O-*pin*ions, in other words – about how you are handling it – not all of them good. For example, one friend's cleaning lady had a fixed idea of how her employer *should* grieve – and show that grief to the world – when the woman's adored husband died. Though the cleaning lady didn't really intend to be critical, she let the widow know she didn't think her demeanor was appropriate. She wanted the widow to be maudlin, to exhibit signs of being perpetually heavy-hearted or angry that things had not gone differently. But the widow, who had struggled with depression throughout much of her life, said that her husband had taught her how to be happy; she viewed an effort to be as upbeat and cheerful as possible as a tribute to the happiness he had given her. She was working hard to be OK; her cleaning lady's attitude was a burden.

Men in particular seem to have a hard time dealing with the conflicting emotions of a death. In a totally unscientific poll that Nancy took among friends and acquaintances who had lost their mothers- or fathers-in-law, all had been blindsided by their husband's anger and fault-finding with everything *they* did immediately following the loss.

> *"My husband was horrible to me for months after his mother died,"* one friend remarked. *"And I don't think he even realized it."*

Regardless of what prompts it – guilt, remorse, sorrow, frustration that you couldn't have done more, this is hard stuff. But the fact that it's hard is evidence that our human connections are precious to us. If those connections didn't matter, this would be easy.

> *"I used to say: "It hurts so good!""* Stephanie says. *"The hurt is part of remembering him."*

Life goes on around you, regardless of how you feel. You will probably have plenty of support initially, but at about the three-months mark, friends may go back to their own complicated lives – and there you are wherever you happen to be with your emotions. When this happens, some people don't know what to do and so they decide: I'll live my life miserably from now on because the person who meant so much to me has died, apparently oblivious of the fact that perpetual mourning is probably *not* what your loved one would have wanted for you.

How do you honor those who have died? By living – not just existing, but truly living while remembering, and sharing stories of the person who has gone. Stories connect us, comfort us, ground us in our lives. They can also help us learn how others have coped with this kind of loss.

People may not approve. They may behave oddly; they may even be dragon-like. Don't let it stop you. Our time here is finite. This three-months' mark is, in some ways, a reminder to you that you need to start putting together your own life in a different way from here on. This is not to say you stop grieving. But, while you still grieve – this process usually takes a long time; it's normal – you also need to keep putting one foot in front of the other. And your friends' gentle retreat back into their own lives is a reminder that we each make our own lives – together to be sure, but we are each responsible for building and maintaining our own individual lives. It's work.

If you are ready to go forward, it does not mean you are leaving the love and the life you shared with the departed behind. It means you are moving into a new chapter that, with some thought and attention, will be informed and enriched by what has past. Gratitude for each emotional gift, each uplift, each warm memory (and even for each hurdle that you will no longer have to jump because of the person and the death) helps enormously.

"I miss him terribly and would give anything to have him back," one widowed friend said, "but I can also eat Thai food again and have a more regular schedule. That's something, anyway."

Get together periodically with your support people. Have wine, beer, tea, conversation, howl at the moon, whatever. The gathering and acknowledging is cathartic. This is partly what memorial services are for—a combination of grieving and gathering a group that is visible proof of what the person meant to others and how he or she connected to other lives in addition to your own. That gathering time can provide you with stories, which often come out in dribs and drabs over the years, stories about the person that will help carry you forward.

Suzanne had lost her husband, and been through breast cancer and colon cancer, but the retired 70+-year-old medical researcher continued to live on her own, raise sheep, train her border collies, swim with friends, have dinner parties, read, and garden – in short, fully live her life until she simply couldn't. When she died, her four middle-aged children, who lived in other states, had all been to see her often in the weeks and days before her death. At the memorial service, friends stood up and shared memories. One man stood up and said that his teenaged son had done odd jobs for Suzanne and discovered that she shared his love of sci-fi books, which meant that when Suzanne came to dinner, the two had plenty of conversation with each other. He talked about how friendship can so easily cross generations when there are shared interests, and about what a gift that was to both his son and to Suzanne. Another of Suzanne's friends, who trained dogs with her, spoke of her integrity, kindness and humor.

"Probably the best person I've ever known," she finished emotionally. Others talked of Suzanne's generosity. When the many people who had loved Susanne finished speaking, her youngest son, with whom she had had a sometimes-rocky relationship, stood up in tears.

"I want to thank you all," he began, haltingly. "I've lived away from my mother for a long time. I always saw her as exacting and distant. I'm sorry I didn't know any of this before, but I'm so grateful to hear it all now. It lets me see her in a different light. It's the picture of her I'll carry with me from now on."

THE SIXTH MONTH HUMP

Many people, who have lost a loved one, particularly a life partner, say that for the first months they felt they were almost on a treadmill, just doing what needed to be done. Friends had rallied and they felt buoyed by the support. But the sixth month is especially hard. Whether it's because what seems like crisis management is over and you must now figure out a life without the person, or because the death feels REAL now, and so unbearably permanent, or because it's when you finally look up and into your own future and can't see what your life could possibly look like without them (or all of the above) is probably moot. Knowing that there may be a wall at six months may not stop you from slamming into it emotionally, but it will keep you from feeling like you're crazy and can help you hold onto the knowledge that you *can* get past it and find joy in life again.

"Grief comes in waves," says Stephanie. "It suddenly completely washes over you; you have no idea where it came from, and you have this terrible anxiety that you're not going to be able to get your head up above it again. You have to tell yourself it comes in waves, and you have to train yourself to understand that that's OK and learn to ride that sensation when it comes."

How grief registers in you and how you express it to the rest of the world depends in part on your temperament as well as the relationship you had with the deceased. You need to heal from this difficult journey – and you can. Give yourself time. Providing care to a terminally ill loved one presents physical and emotional challenges even after they are gone. There will be times when you feel stuck in neutral, when you feel there is no point now that that person is gone.

"He was my person for twenty-five years," says Esther. "The one person I talked to every day, and told everything to. I counted on him. And as time goes on, it's getting harder, not easier. It's begun to really sink in that he's not coming back, and I'm having a hard time figuring out what to do with my life now."

You are not alone.

You may feel alternately numb and then overcome with emotion at the most unexpected times. Someone can offer a simple word of condolence and you break down without warning. Simple things – a book; card; phrase; piece of clothing; strain of music; the smell of lilac blossoms or vegetable soup – can catapult you back to a different time in your life, and bring on a wave of longing and sorrow. The triggers are many. One friend said she dreaded going to her son's soccer game because it would be held on the same field that the helicopter that had carried her mother away when she was dying had taken off from.

Don't be reluctant to seek grief counseling. We are social animals; knowing we are part of a group whose members experience many of the same struggles and sorrows, that others have gone through this and learned how to move forward offers some comfort. Counselors, too, can help you with the acceptance of your loss, which will help you to build your life without the person. Accepting the loss is the beginning of learning how to step into a new chapter.

Whoever you have lost, you have been dealing with grief through this entire ordeal. You watched the disease chip away your loved one's strength, stamina, appetite, independence, and at the ways you shared your lives. Each step along the way forced another adjustment, getting used to another new normal for both your dying loved one and for you as caregiver. And you will in all likelihood, continue to grieve one way or another. But take heart: time will gradually soften the pain.

Chapter Thirteen

NOW, PUSH *FORWARD*

This is your opportunity to assess how that death – and life – went. It's a difficult exercise, but also a strengthening and cathartic one. Are there things you learned from this experience that will change how you go forward with your own life?

One friend who lost her husband in her early forties, said that when she finally 'came up for air,' she made a decision about how she wanted to make choices from then on.

"I thought: I want to be conscious of what I let into my life," she told us. "I don't have time any more for things that sap my energy and give back nothing. I don't want to spend time with people who are only about them. I don't want to spend my life with negativity. I want to really live and live well."

Moving forward means not allowing the inner critic to keep you stuck and spinning your wheels on all the possibilities that *could* have been. Will this be a seamless transition? Doubtful. You may take two steps forward and one step back. One day you're good, the next day you're a mess. Go easy on yourself and continue to move forward. Start small, treat yourself to a nice carryout or if you feel like sitting in a restaurant, ask a friend to join you. Buy a new houseplant; take a walk. Outside, in nature, you might be amazed at how differently you begin to look at life around you. Consciously create new routines. Begin to cheer for yourself: after going through a terminal illness with a loved one you can handle just about anything.

Martha had driven to Ohio with her terminally ill husband of 41 years to share Thanksgiving with longtime friends. Thanksgiving morning, her husband died there in bed next to her. She had to make arrangements to ship his body home then drive the 900 miles back home retracing the miles without him. A year later, she told us: "I think he'd like me better now. I'm so much more capable than when I depended on him for everything!"

Somewhere around the sixth month following her husband's death, Stephanie, who says she had not written a word during the whole fourteen months of her husband's illness, took up her pen.

"I think things had been working in the background," she says, " even though I was completely unable to write the whole time I was going through it with him. But gradually, I regained my ability to write again...and that gave me a sense of repair and focus."

To help you move forward you may want to talk about the deceased and share your experience. It not only validates how you managed, it helps you explore your feelings then and now. This may be a good time to join a bereavement group. A bereavement group can give you the opportunity to discuss this loss with people who may be feeling much the same as you do. Check with your community, religious affiliate, or local hospice. If your loved one was involved in hospice care, bereavement groups are generally free; if you were not in a program most offer a sliding payment scale. Hospice programs 'get it;' and can offer much-needed support, especially in the first months. They will generally maintain some kind of agreed-to contact for the entire first year to help you through 'all the firsts' – holidays, birthdays, anniversaries – following a death.

TIP: If you were involved in a hospice program but have returned home or moved to a different state most programs will set you up with a hospice bereavement program in your state.

Slowly you will begin to re-evaluate your own life, including choosing which battles (if any) you want to fight and which to let go, which people you want to keep close and which you want to keep at a distance. Put a hold on those who drain you. Think about how you want to go forward into your next chapter.

Begin to rebuild:

- Don't say: I can't. Say: I'll try.
- Don't wallow in regrets.
- You did your best.
- Be proud of what you overcame.
- Be proud of what you accomplished.
- Laughter is good; it's not disrespectful to the deceased.
- Ask yourself: How would they want you to live?
- Honor them *by living*.
- What did you learn from this experience?
- Chose to grow from the experience.
- What have you learned about living?
- How can you make your own parting easier for those you leave behind?

Watching someone die can lessen fears and anxieties. You may not be ready to catch the next bus out to The Great Beyond, but you can look at death through different eyes. Obviously you are NOT okay with their dying

but eventually, after enough time has passed, (however long 'enough' is) you *will* be okay and go on living with fond memories of what you shared in life.

You know you are making progress when:

- You return to work.
- You're feeling hopeful.
- You feel you've regained some control over your emotions and your life.
- You discover new capabilities you never realized you had (before this experience).
- You can make plans for the future.

BUT, don't push yourself too hard. Shortly after her husband died, Stephanie, a musician as well as a poet, tried to join an organization that plays music for the dying. The organization turned her down.

> *"It was too soon and they knew it,"* she says.

Chapter Fourteen

Poet Seamus Heany's last words were: *Do not be afraid.*

STAY OPEN

This is a really tough transition, but it's a normal transition. We will all go through losing a loved one – maybe even our special person – at some time in our lives. It's really hard. Our human connections, so piercing and deep, will inevitably be severed as we know them here. Which is perhaps what makes those connections and the day-to-day appreciation of them so vital. Grieving that loss, however that manifests – and for each person it takes a different trajectory – is an important and unavoidable part of our life's experience.

We grieve the way we live (just as we die the way we live). The way each of us feels and expresses grief is determined by our temperaments, our circumstances, and the relationship we had with the person who died.

> *Carla sat by Brad's bedside until he breathed his last. She honored his choices in that agonizing journey, regardless of whether she agreed with them or not. Hers was the loss of a beloved son and friend, who had finally 'gotten himself together.' She mourned him deeply. But it did not stop her from moving forward in her own life. She spoke of him often with love and sometimes sadness, but at the same time, she put her own paperwork in order for the time of her own death. She made conscious efforts to connect with people, volunteered as a mentor, worked in a job that fulfilled her need for both income and purpose, and, after many years as a divorcee, found love and married again.*
>
> *"I've had a lot of fun in my life," she says. "There's been a lot of sadness too, but I've had a lot of fun."*

Because Nancy and her mother believed so strongly in life beyond the grave, the sadness of losing someone she was very close to, and who had been such a large part of her days and those of her children, was mitigated by her conviction that her mother's spirit had not died. That belief was buttressed by a dream she had.

> *"A couple of days after Mom died, Dad and I were taking a walk and he said there was so much he wished he had said to her. He was talking about what my brother and I call unfinished business. My brother and I were fortunate, because neither of us felt that way about our relationships with Mom. I said: "I just wish I could hug her once more to say goodbye."*
>
> *"That night, I had a dream," she says. "It was dim all around me. [In the dream] I was sitting on the curb outside my uncle's house changing a tire, and I could feel*

someone standing near my left shoulder. I looked up and saw my mom standing there with a big smile on her face. I asked her what she was doing there."

"You called me," she said

"I wanted one last hug."

"I know. You are so silly," she responded, and reached out her arms.

"I stood up, and she gave me a hug so long and so firm, that I could feel it while I was lying in bed dreaming. The funny thing is, I knew even while I was dreaming that it was a dream, but I could feel it in my sleeping body. And it helped."

Sue's reassuring experience was while she was wide awake.

"It had been eighteen months since my father died," she says. "I walked into my living room early in the morning to look out the window that overlooked the valley and check on the weather. Suddenly, a strong scent of my dad's cologne grabbed my intention. I remember softly saying out loud, "Dad?" I slowly turned from the window to... what? See him? Hear him? His scent left as quickly as it had come, but it left me feeling excited, even giddy. I was happy that he had made his presence known. I am, after all, a veteran hospice nurse and have witnessed and heard from many patients who have had experiences with deceased relatives. This was my own experience of my dad, brief as it was. It left me full of joy. I won't pretend to define what any of that episode meant — so far no one has come back to tell me what any of this means — but this I do know: it left me with a peaceful calmness."

One woman, who had worked throughout the marriage, lost her husband of 40 years. She assumed that work would be her only focus for the next chapter in her life, which she imagined to be spent alone. Then she met a man, a widower who had lost his wife of many years several years before. They married.

"When Jim died, I thought I'd never be happy again," she told us. "But I am. And I'm so grateful!"

If the person was your primary confidant, you probably feel a huge void in your life and wonder if you will ever find someone you can confide in that way again. If they were the reason you got up and made breakfast, put on makeup, shaved, you may wonder why you want to bother. If they were the primary breadwinner, or the financial planner, you may be feeling overwhelmed by the responsibility of making financial decisions on your own. You are grieving while also learning how to live without them. This is normal. (We know we've said this a lot, but it's true, and it's not bad to have a reminder).

Twelve years after her husband's death, Stephanie has rebuilt her life. She is training to offer music therapy for hospice patients in the same organization that turned her down immediately after her husband's death. She remembers the loss but it's no longer the gaping wound it once was.

"I think about him a lot," she says, "but it's not with the same pain. And I know how much my music meant to my husband when he was dying. Now I'm really ready to give that to someone else."

You've reached another new normal. Acceptance does not mean you will forget them or what they meant to you.

LET THE MEMORIES COME

Anything can spark a memory. Proust's madeleine cookies prompted him to write an entire book on the mundane but important memories in his life. Your memory triggers may be anything from the smell of wood shavings, bourbon, onion soup or diesel fuel to the sound of the front door opening, passing the hospital where your loved one last stayed or the apartment you once shared to hearing her favorite song, or seeing the emblem of his favorite football team or a picture of Snoopy like the one he had tattooed on his back. Memories will come when you least expect it – doing the dishes, riding down the road when the song that you hated and he loved comes on the radio, at a meeting when you hear the same words come out of your own mouth that used to come out of his or hers, at a joke, walking the dog, pumping gas in the car, taking a shower, looking out a window. At first they may be painful or bittersweet. You may even feel angry at their being gone and wish some of those memories weren't so embedded and connected with the person. Holidays and annual milestones – birthdays, anniversaries – can be especially difficult. It's all normal. Finding new ways to commemorate (or ignore) these milestones will help. So will time. Time softens the hard edges of experience and helps us to enjoy remembering the sweet or funny or ironic things.

- The way the screen door slammed when he came home from work
- The way the corner of her mouth curled when she smiled
- The way he lit up a room just by showing up
- The careful way she dressed for working in her garden – polyester pants suit, hair coiffed and makeup on
- The precision he used to open a steamed crab
- The way she could just look at you and know that both knew what the other was thinking
- The way she always 'let the roots know who's boss' when planting a shrub
- The way he barreled and tore through life

- The way he always listened when you most needed him to
- The way he stacked the firewood or did fifty other little chores around the house as a way to say *I love you.*
- The way she always remembered to phone on your birthday

These simple memories – everyone has his or her own specific list – can be like welcome postcards from your shared past. They can remind you of what is no longer there, yes, but also of those small things that connected you and made up the fabric of your time together. One wife of only five years saved all of the little Post-It notes her husband had left for her each morning before going off to work. She looks at a few each day. They remind her of the love that she feels blessed to have had, though it was not nearly as long as either had a reason to expect. Those notes also remind her that the man she loved "would have wanted us to go on in a good way, enjoying our lives and helping other people."

And, if you experience things like the smell of the person's cologne, a dream, or, as one three-year-old grandson says he did one morning, a visit from his dead grandmother that included a conversation with her about how much she loved him, count it as a gift.

We're not trying to convince you that spirit, a life of the soul that transcends the physical life we lose here, is real. We've had enough evidence to be persuaded of it ourselves, but we also know that experiencing something yourself is far more convincing than hearing about it. (And even then, some will find it impossible to credit). But we *are* suggesting that it helps to be open to some of the invisible gifts (we would say spiritual gifts, but whatever you want to call them) that can come not long after someone you love has died. They can be incredibly reassuring and comforting. One son (a state legislator, as it happens) believed firmly that once the body dies: that's it. Yet, after sitting with his father at the moment of death, he says he saw his father's soul leave his body, which told him that there is something more beyond this corporeal life. (This, we believe, is also what makes ghost stories so compelling, the evidence of life beyond the grave). Can we prove any of this? No. But hospice workers, whose job is to watch death on a nearly daily basis, manage to find joy as well as satisfaction in their nearness to this ultimate transition in life. They often use the term 'privileged' when they talk about being there at the moment someone dies.

"People ask us how we do this work," says one hospice chaplain. "Some people wonder whether there is life after death. We know there is."

Whether you believe this or not, is not so much the point. If there is life beyond, hooray! If not, we won't know it. Ultimately, our time here, together, is what matters most.

This has been a difficult, painful journey. You may want to run away, or attempt to wall yourself off from the grief. But by shutting those emotional doors completely, you may be missing some of the blessings it has to offer. It also offers an opportunity to examine our own lives through the prism of what we've just experienced – as Linda who became a hospice nurse, did following the death of her father – and make some conscious decisions going forward.

WHERE DO WE GO FROM HERE?

Most of us can choose how we approach life. Yes, temperament and circumstance influence some of it, but you can choose how to respond to many of the obstacles and sorrows as well as joys and successes in life. You can choose to remain stuck and angry that death is ultimately unavoidable. You can choose to give up your own pleasures in what we consider a misguided attempt to honor the person you've lost. For example, one father vowed to give up golf, his passion, when his artist son died. The son hadn't even played golf. Yet abstaining from a sport he loved was a sacrifice that the father felt would somehow honor his son. Or maybe he thought he shouldn't have fun since his son could no longer enjoy things here, or perhaps it was some kind of personal penance he was doing to atone for surviving his son. Is that what Keith, who desperately wanted to live and to continue to create, would have wanted for his father's remaining life here? Unlikely. You're already hurting. Forgoing something that you enjoy is not going to help the person who's gone. It will only hurt you more.

Of course you *can* choose to give up your own pleasure. Or, you can do what a friend, who deeply grieved the loss of her young husband, did. She grieved, wailed in the night and was desperately unhappy that their time together had been cut so short. But she also looked carefully at her life and made some conscious decisions.

Jessie was only 37 when her husband died. He had been her great love, her partner in life and in business; his death from cancer was relatively swift and completely unexpected. She was devastated. Her entire life had crumbled just at an age when many people begin to feel as though the foundation has been laid for a long and happy life together. She couldn't concentrate; work following his death was a daily struggle. But as devastated as she felt, she also knew that she had to make a conscious effort to turn the corner into another chapter in her own life. And she was (and still is) quite beautiful, energetic and smart. She began to examine the job, the business, the living situation, the people she knew and spent time with through the prism of how each affected her. She looked at which were positive and which were negative influences on her emotions, her spirit, and her daily existence. And she decided to make changes.

"I always kind of knew, but was really clear after that about how short life is," she says now.

Jessie, who had no children, began dating. One man in particular wanted her to become a suburban housewife and bear his children. Her friends were having children, giving parties, joining clubs and living what many consider to be the ideal suburban life. But after long consideration, Jessie realized that that was not the life she wanted for herself. She also realized that she had a choice. She eventually married an older man, who is now both her creative partner and a person who understands that building a life takes courage, vision and conscious effort. She will never be the suburban wife and mother. And that's just fine.

"There was a time when I could have had children, and I thought a long time before I cut off that option, but in the end I made a conscious choice not to, and it was the right one for me," she says now. She teaches and pursues her art with the love and support of her husband.

A proactive approach to this huge turning point is what we've been advocating all along. Part of being proactive is examining your own life honestly and with a sense of going forward in the best way you can, experiencing and sharing all the joy (which is slightly different from happiness) that comes your way and that you can create for yourself and for others. Life here is much bigger and broader and fuller than most of us are able to see while we are racing through it.

Where you go from here depends on a host of factors, but most important among them are: who was the person to you, what are your circumstances, and who are you as a person?

Some of this is attitude; some is individual temperament. Some people are wired to forge ahead, others struggle to meet each day, and most of us do something in between. Sometimes it's as though we can't walk out of the house without the person who is gone. At other times, we're astonishingly grateful to be alive to witness a sunset, a friend's wedding, share a conversation with someone new. Yet even with this sense of being on an emotional rollercoaster, we can still make choices in our lives, whether the choices are easier and more natural for some than for others does not mean we cannot choose. And we should do so with an eye to making our lives and the lives of those around us as good as they can be.

This next chapter in your life will take time and conscious effort to construct if the person was an enormous part of your days. One friend, whose husband died after a 42-year marriage that had begun in college, said it took her five years to learn how to live alone. But she has, beautifully, with great gusto and benefit to those around her. 'A sparkle' is how one of her friends describes her now.

There are many decisions that will face you that you may not be accustomed to making or at least making alone. It can be overwhelming at first, but as with most things, as you practice, it will get easier.

This experience can be a catalyst for making positive changes in your life and the way you plan to approach its end, given what you've learned. Easy? No. Possible? Definitely. If you want to be OK (and sometimes even if you don't) you most likely will be in time.

One positive step you can take is to reflect on what you believe you will want for yourself. This is your opportunity to assess how that death went, and how you want to approach your own, at least as much as you can. None of us, unless we are born with a life-limiting illness or condition, really has a clue about where or how we will meet our own death. (And even then, we could be in for a surprise).

Regardless of whatever is in store for you and the two of us and our loved ones and everyone else on this earth, there are things we can put into place now that may well help us in our own journey and will help those we leave behind.

You can talk with the people closest to you – whether that's your spouse or significant other, your parents, your children or your closest friends, about what you want for yourself. And you can WRITE IT ALL DOWN. For those with a family that's not always harmonious (we can't imagine what that would be like since we come from incredibly perfect families and incredibly perfect relationships!), think through what each person might inherit or who might wish for some memento of the times you shared, and what you want to leave with them. And write it down. Nancy's mother one day showed Nancy a cut glass dish that had been her grandmother's. "I want this to go to Kay," she told Nancy. Kay was a member of her mother's church, and a daughter-like friend to Nancy's mother. The morning her mother died, Nancy called Kay and made sure that she got the dish that would, each time Kay used it, remind her of the friendship, the mutual support and the laughter the two friends had shared. That gift to Kay was also a gift to Nancy the day her mother died; Nancy was able to share her own grief with someone who cared deeply and who could commiserate from a place of genuine sorrow. Nancy's mother didn't write it down, (though she wrote down most of it). But it's simpler, and you won't have to worry about the cut glass dish or the humidor, or the favorite baseball cap, fishing rod, silver baby spoon or whatever getting lost in the sadness and flurry of activity that follows a death if you write it all down.

Then put it with all your other important papers. Make a will, fill out a medical directive, and consider, depending on your age and circumstances, giving someone trusted and trustworthy a power of attorney.

You've just gone through this intimate experience with death. There is nothing routine about it, despite its inevitability. You may be forever changed – our lives change us as we live them. Yet this difficult journey makes life itself more precious and more real.

Stephanie's husband had a little cabin that he'd built. He had spent every evening there.

"For a long, long time, I couldn't bear to go back," she says now. "The cabin was falling down. My stepson would say: 'That house is a corpse,' which was very painful. But twelve years later, a bunch of us spent a summer renovating it; it was the ultimate intervention [for me and for the house]. We preserved everything that felt like it was imbued with his spirit, but we made everything in the place operational again. For me that was a great release and turned the grief into something constructive."

The cabin is now rented to a young artist. Having someone else in that space was, even after all those years, a difficult transition for Stephanie, but she recognizes that it is also a good one.

"A house needs to be lived-in," she says. "And I'm glad that it's lived in by someone who will appreciate it."

Regardless of what you believe, whether you are convinced there is life beyond this one or not, what matters most is to remain open and present to *being* in our lives, and truly *with* those with whom we share them. This time, with all its complications, its heartaches and joys, is what we have together.

IN TIME WHAT REALLY MATTERS is that you were *there*. You were present. You did your best under difficult circumstances, and that effort, however imperfect, however difficult, is an act of love that made a difference to your loved one and to you. None of us is getting out of here alive. We are all, one way or another, walking each other home.

CHECKLISTS

Where To Start (Paperwork and Practicalities, Chapter 2)

o   Sign documents
o   Power of Attorney
o   Medical power of attorney
o   Living Will
o   HIPAA
o   Who is the primary caregiver
o   Who can help out weekly, biweekly, monthly
o   Who can provide caregiver respite
o   Who can help with errands
o   Who can help with transportation
o   Who can provide meals
o   If your loved one needs electricity to power life-support equipment in their home such as respirators, etc., some electric companies offer the Emergency Medical Equipment Notification Program. Check it the electric company

Stocking The Sick Room (Chapter 5)

o   4 extra pillows
o   Box bendable straws
o   Rubber sheet
o   Disposable gloves
o   Adult pull ups
o   Barrier Cream
o   Natural tears

Caregiver Survival/Emergency Kit for Outages/Storms

- o Flashlights and extra batteries
- o Battery/hand crank portable NOAA weather or regular radio
- o Fire extinguisher
- o Fill car tank with gas if bad weather is predicted
- o Get cash
- o Have extra car keys
- o Have extra house keys
- o Have extra tanks portable oxygen delivered before a bad storm
- o Multipurpose tool (screwdriver, knife, etc.)
- o First aide kit for cuts/injuries
- o Hand sanitizer
- o Antiseptic wipes
- o extra hearing aid batteries, eyeglasses, syringes
- o Fill bath tub with water to use for flushing toilet
- o Stock extra bottles of water for drinking /cleaning
- o Stock plastic utensils, cups, plates
- o Stock extra box disposable gloves, dust mask if appropriate
- o Stock extra toilet paper, & garbage bags
- o Stock up with can nourishment, power bars, nuts, and granola
- o Have extra blankets, sleeping bags for warmth
- o Whistle
- o Car charger for cell phone
- o Have prescriptions, meds refilled

If You Must Travel by Car

- o In addition to items listed above
- o Bring copy of DNR
- o Bring copy of Advanced Directives
- o Bring all current medicines
- o Make sure you have a cell phone charger for the car

FOOD FOR THOUGHT- RECIPES

Nancy, who is also a food writer, organic gardener and cook, has included what she hopes will be a few easy-to-follow recipes and ideas for providing delicious, economical and healthy meals for yourself as caregiver and potentially for your loved one.

BEEF:

It's What's for Dinner. It's probably a DNA cue from our hunter-gatherer roots. The minute the weather turns cooler, we start thinking about more substantial meals, a yearning to bulk up for what in our species' earlier days were winter's hunger months. We want something that will stick to the ribs for more than the time it takes to digest a bit of sushi or a salad, something that could, if need be, carry us through an entire day and into the next.

Pot roast with potatoes, carrots and onions, stroganoff, or beef stew with rutabaga, turnips and celery are quick and easy to prepare, but offer substantial nourishment. In addition to the mouthwatering aromas you enjoy while the stuff is cooking, pot roasts and stews use the cheap cuts – chuck, arm roast, crosscut shanks and others – so they're economical.

Pot roast and beef stew recipes abound. They run the gamut from the simplest meaty bones (leftover or not) flung into a casserole with some vegetables and water and either popped into the oven or simmered on the stove to the more complicated but luscious boeuf bourguignon (burgundy beef stew). These meals are also very forgiving. If you have to stop in the middle of prepping, it doesn't matter. If you have to turn it off for a couple of hours while it's cooking and come back to it, it will be just as delicious as if you'd hovered over it.

Two great kitchen tools: a heavy iron pot that works either on top of the stove or in the oven; and a slow-cooker/Crockpot, which is a godsend for a working person who loves to eat well without putting in tons of time.

For stew base: rough chop two carrots, two ribs of celery, and two onions. Sauté in olive oil or canola oil for about five minutes. Salt and pepper. Add a pound or two of cubed beef and brown for about five minutes more. (You could instead use ground beef for this and leave the big chunks intact as it browns). Add a heaping tablespoon of flour and stir for five minutes. Pour in enough liquid – water or broth or a combination of water and red wine or maybe dark beer – to cover everything. Then add a 15 oz. can of chopped tomatoes, some sage or thyme, maybe a little coriander or cardamom. Cover and simmer for about an hour and a half, or pop it into a 325F oven until the meat's tender (about an hour). Check it once about halfway through in case it needs more liquid.

Stew can be tweaked in all kinds of ways to please even the pickiest of eaters. Use any kind of meat -- pork, chicken, beef, lamb, duck, goose, venison, fish, or even squirrel, rabbit, or muskrat (these last three are Ye Olde Eastern Shore of Maryland staples). You can easily make a couple of different stews on a Sunday afternoon. Serve one that night, and another later in the week. Use what's left of one as base for soup by adding liquid, more veggies, maybe a can or two of beans, and a little more seasoning. Serve with crusty bread, biscuits, or cornbread and salad. Guinness, port or red wine are nice liquid additions to 'red' meat (lamb, beef, venison). For venison, add a little red currant jelly too. Variations on stew are endless. White wine, cider, light beer are good liquid additions for chicken, fish or other light meat.

English chef Jamie Oliver lived in West Virginia teaching the time-and-energy-challenged locals how to cook easily and eat well and healthily. He understands the American yearning for beef coupled with the need for variety and ease. Below are links to recipes to get you started.

http://allrecipes.com//Recipe/slow-cooker-beef-stew-i/Detail.aspx
http://www.foodnetwork.com/recipes/tyler-florence/the-ultimate-beef-stew-recipe2/index.html
http://www.countrycrock.com/recipes/detail/11708/1/argentinian-beef-stew

For a pot roast, start with a little olive oil or canola oil in the pot, sear the meat on both sides, add some chopped veggies as above, but instead of cubed meat, use a blade roast, arm roast, chuck roast, bottom round roast or top round roast. Any of the cheaper cuts will do. Add the liquid, and whatever herbs or spices your heart desires and simmer for about 45 minutes. Then add a couple of peeled potatoes if you like, and simmer for another half hour or until the potatoes are tender. In the last few minutes, you could add green beans or peas, frozen lima beans or something on that order. Serve it with a green salad and maybe a glass of red wine or beer.

Cassoulet (of course, it's French) is a versatile meat-and-bean casserole perfect for a slow cooker or a casserole in the oven. Originally, French cooks used potted goose or duck, pork and sausage as the meat. I often use lamb shanks or beef cross-cut shanks. Brown the shanks (or whatever other meat you use), then put them in a casserole with canned navy beans, red wine, garlic, onions, thyme, parsley, a large tin of tomatoes, maybe a juniper berry or two, a beef bullion cube, salt and pepper. Cover and let it cook slowly (3 hours or so; you'll need to add some liquid probably halfway through). It's done when the beans are soft and the meat is falling off the bone. Comforting.

CHICKEN:

You can buy a rotisserie chicken or two at the supermarket or roast your own. Chicken makes a great easy dinner and yields leftovers for a host of one-skillet suppers later in the week. AND roasting a chicken makes a place -- apartment, house, mansion or trailer -- smell like home and gives you (or at least many of us), a sense of wellbeing, even in the face of difficult times.

To Roast A Chicken: Take one whole chicken. For more leftovers use two whole chickens. Wash, dry, and put in a roasting pan loosely stuffed with part of an onion, the leafy tops of some celery and a carrot. Salt and pepper the outsides. Ring the chicken(s) with a couple of whole or halved peeled onions, some potatoes, carrots and turnips – your veggies for this meal. Cover and shove into the oven at 350F for something like two hours. The old wives' rule of thumb for when a chicken is done is 'when the juices run clear when you poke a fork into the thigh meat.' Another general guide is 20 minutes of roasting time per pound of bird. The meat thermometer should read at least 165 degrees F. Either Google 'chicken roasting times' or look them up in Joy of Cooking or any other decent basic cookbook for more precise timing.

http://www.cooking.com/Recipes-and-More/recipes/Simple-Roast-Chicken-recipe-9473.aspx.

With very little time and effort, you have a delicious meal.

After supper, take the remaining meat off the bones – it takes maybe ten minutes -- and store it in the fridge. Or, if you don't have the energy that night, once you've finished supper, stick the bird still in the roasting pan into the fridge; tomorrow, take off the meat and make stock.

With leftover meat (which is why you roasted two birds) you can easily throw together any or all of a host of things: curried chicken and rice (sautéed onions, celery, carrots, chopped chicken seasoned with curry powder, Worcestershire, salt and pepper with a little chicken stock added); Chicken pot pie (cooked carrots, onions, and frozen peas in herby chicken stock thickened with a little cornstarch; put it into a casserole, top with a crust and bake at 350 for about 45 minutes); chicken fajitas (sauté onion, sweet pepper, jalapeno, add the cubed chicken, black olives, tomatoes, chili powder, garlic, cumin, cilantro and wrap in a tortilla), or make the chicken version of tuna noodle casserole….well, you get the idea.

(http://allrecipes.com/Recipe/Chicken-And-Apple-Curry/Detail.aspx)

http://allrecipes.com/recipe/chicken-pot-pie-ix/

http://www.foodandwine.com/recipes/easy-chicken-fajitas

http://www.campbellskitchen.com/recipes/hearty-chicken-noodle-casserole-50682

One of the best ways to save money, make good use of every last bit of food you've paid for and feed yourself well is to make soup. Besides, as A.A. Milne's Christopher Robin said: 'soup is a comforting sort of thing to have.' Soup can be simple, economical, delicious and nutritious, and can be made with almost anything you have in the fridge – leftover cooked veggies, that last onion or carrot, a couple of green beans that didn't get eaten, leftover rice, leftover mashed potatoes, whatever. You can even boil stock and whisk a raw egg and a handful of spinach into it for a lightning-quick, nutritious meal.

Soup starts with stock.

For Stock of Almost Any Kind:

Take the roasted remains of whatever – ham bone, beef shin bones, oxtail – and put them in a large pot. Add a couple of carrots, a stalk or just the tops of celery, a large onion, quartered, some thyme if you have it, maybe a bay leaf, and about a teaspoon of salt and pepper for every two quarts of water. (You can season the soup later if you don't find it salty enough). Then add plenty of water (the rule of thumb is to add enough water to cover the whole lot by about an inch and a half).

To Make Chicken Stock: Use a stockpot or big soup pot. Throw the carcass, skin, neck, the stuffing veggies and the richly-flavored 'fond' (the scrapings) on the bottom of the roasting pan (pour a little hot water in to scrape up all the bits) into the stockpot. Or start the stock in the roasting pan itself if it will safely go on the burner. Add half an onion, celery tops, and a carrot or two, some thyme, parsley, maybe tarragon, salt, pepper and plenty of water to cover. Simmer for an hour while you're doing something

else. Stick the stock in the fridge to cool before you go to bed. Next evening, skim off and discard the fat (or give it to the cat), take out bones, etc. (Another ten minutes' work, tops). What's left is beautiful fresh stock.

Stock aka broth freezes well and is like money in the bank. Put it into pint or quart containers (be sure to label them), and stack them in the freezer. When you want something good but have very little energy and time, you can pull out a container, and put it into a lidded pot set on low heat. It will defrost while you pull a few things out of the fridge to add – a potato and some cheese, or peppers, leftover rice (or uncooked rice that will cook in the broth) and some leftover meat, or a can of beans and some garlic and parsley and a squeeze of lemon. In no time flat, you have a real meal that costs, depending on ingredients, as little as a buck or two for a couple of people. Add bread, a salad, (a glass of wine if you like) and you've got something that will nourish the body and the spirit.

Soup possibilities are endless. Mom's chicken noodle (aka Jewish penicillin), broccoli and parmesan, butternut with apple and onion, cream of celery or cream of any other veg, cauliflower with mushrooms and gorgonzola, leek and potato, tortilla soup with peppers and tomatoes – basically, whatever you've got on hand can go into the soup pot.

There's a good reason virtually every culture on earth makes soup. Oxtail, gumbo, bouillabaisse, split pea, albondigas with pork and beef meatballs, stracciatella, an Italian egg drop soup that you can make in about ten minutes, harvest corn chowder with bacon, Scotch broth with barley, oyster stew with thyme and sautéed onions, clam chowder, salmon and potato chowder, duck and tortilla soup, green bean and bacon with orzo and herbs, Thai shrimp and noodles, old-fashioned chicken noodle, cabbage soup with sausage, borscht.

Having soup in the fridge is a great lunch option, too. Once a week take some to work in a microwaveable container instead of snacking on salt-and-sugar-laden carbs. One of my lunch favorites is quick but elegant: Cauliflower soup with mushrooms and blue cheese. Dump two cups of fresh cauliflower into six cups of beef broth. Add a large chopped shallot, about six mushrooms, some thyme, dash of nutmeg, and simmer. When vegetables are cooked (about 20 minutes), puree or mash with a potato masher. At the end, stir in a big dollop of whole yogurt and about 1/3 cup of broken up Stilton or other hard blue cheese. (Brie's good too).

To Make Vegetarian Stock: Simply put a bunch of vegetables (be sure to include onion, celery and carrot) into a stockpot with plenty of water, maybe a bay leaf, some crushed garlic, and a little salt and pepper.

Simmer for about an hour, cool, and drain off the liquid to use as a soup base.

Roasted sweet potato soup with poblanos, peasant lentil vegetable, leek and potato, Ghanaian peanut soup, Swiss cheese and onion, Hungarian mushroom (you can use tamari sauce to add the kind of umami – pronounced Oooo, Mommy! – savory flavor that a beef stock imparts), vegetable chowder with milk, creamy roasted parsnip, carrot and turnip with a drizzle of lemon juice and fresh parsley, eggplant and mushroom with sautéed sweet pepper, Tuscan bean with tomatoes and kale, roasted tomato-and-onion.

Soup -- and rest and laughter, which often go hand in hand with soup -- helps recharge batteries. The aroma of simmering soup is encouraging, a visceral signal that despite economical downturns, setbacks, hard times and downright failures, we can go on.

A FEW SOUP RECIPES:

Mulligatawny soup:

Chicken stock. Add an apple, peeled and cut into quarters, a 15-oz tin of tomatoes, a carrot, some leftover chicken if you've got it, maybe some lima beans, corn. Put in anywhere from a teaspoon to a tablespoon of curry powder, depending on your taste, and a good splash (like a tablespoon) of Worcestershire sauce. Simmer until the vegetables are tender.

Mexican Squash Soup

2 tblsp butter or olive oil
1 small onion, chopped
¼ cup chopped celery
¼ cup sweet pepper, chopped
4 cups chicken or vegetable stock
1 dried red Mexican chili or 1 fresh Serrano or other hot pepper to taste, whole (optional).
1 ½ cups peeled, diced winter squash (acorn, Hubbard, butternut, etc.)
1 cup frozen or fresh corn

Melt butter or heat oil in saucepan. Sauté vegetables until soft, about 5 minutes. Add stock and bring to boil. Add squash and simmer until tender. Puree.

Roasted Sweet Potato and Poblano

2 sweet potatoes, peeled and cubed
1 tblsp smoked paprika
1 tblsp chili powder
1 tsp cumin
1 tsp salt
1 tsp pepper
2 tblsp olive oil
1 shallot minced
1 med poblano pepper, chopped
1 tblsp olive oil
4 cups chicken stock or 4 cups water and a large chicken bullion cube
3 tblsp fresh cilantro

Toss cubed potatoes with spices and olive oil. Roast on a cookie sheet at 325F for about 30 minutes or until semi-tender. Sauté shallot (or onion) and poblano in olive oil until onion is translucent and some of the peppers have some browned edges. Put all into a soup pot with stock or water and bullion and simmer for about 15 minutes. Puree with a hand blender or cool a bit before putting it into the blender. To serve, top with chopped fresh cilantro.

Minestrone

½ lb meaty bacon
3 tblsp olive oil
2 carrots, chopped
1 turnip, chopped
2 onions, chopped
2 ribs celery, chopped
4 cloves garlic, minced
3 large tomatoes or 1 15-oz tin chopped tomatoes with juice
1 cup green beans, chopped
½ cup sweet pepper. diced
3 tblsp fresh oregano, minced
3 tblsp fresh parsley, minced
1 15-oz. can cannellini beans or 2 cups of dried beans that have been soaked then simmered until al dente
1 cup elbow macaroni
7-8 cups beef stock
salt and pepper to taste

Use a large, heavy pot for this – enameled iron works well. Heat olive oil in pot while you slice bacon into inch-long pieces. Sauté the bacon in hot olive oil until not quite crisp. If there is too much fat in the pan, spoon some out. Meanwhile, cube/dice the carrots, turnip, onions, and celery and add to the hot fat-and-oil. Sauté for about 10 minutes until vegetables are starting to brown slightly on edges. Add garlic and sauté for another minute. Then add tomatoes, sweet pepper, green beans, herbs and stock. If using plumped dried beans, add them now. Simmer for about 40 minutes. If using canned beans, add them after the initial vegetables are tender, and also add the macaroni. Cook for about 15 minutes or until pasta is done, stirring to keep things from sticking to the bottom. You may need to add liquid by this point, though this soup is thick. Serve with crusty garlic bread and robust red wine.

http://allrecipes.com/Recipe/mulligatawny-soup-i/detail.aspx
http://www.care2.com/greenliving/peasant-lentil-vegetable-soup.html
http://allrecipes.com/Recipe/african-peanut-soup/detail.aspx
http://www.marthastewart.com/318061/vegetable-chowder
http://glutenfreegoddess.blogspot.com/2008/10/roasted-vegetable-chowder.html
Kosher soups:
http://kosherfood.about.com/od/koshersouprecipes/Kosher_Soup_Recipes.htm
http://www.kosherdelight.com/Soups.shtml

HAM:

Ham is rich in both taste and texture, so a little goes a long way. One cup of cured whole ham is 206 calories, according to caloriecount.com. Be aware that cured ham has lots of sodium -- over 2100 mg in a one-cup serving. So if water retention is a problem you might want to stay away from ham.

If the salt isn't a problem, a ham offers a lot of options for meals. Cut cubes of ham for ham and cheese and potato casserole with cream of celery soup. Pare the last bits off the bone for use in quiche along with sautéed peppers and onions or asparagus with tarragon and Swiss cheese. You can easily make ham omelets or baked eggs with ham and chives. Ham salad (chopped ham with some mustard and mayo and chopped sweet pickle) on crackers or in a sandwich, grilled ham and cheese and tomato sandwiches, ham and asparagus quiche, or simply sauté ham with crab or ham with mushrooms to put on pasta. Top with a little grated cheese.

Ham Casserole

Mix together in a casserole dish:
2 cups or so of cooked cubed potatoes
1½ cups of diced ham
1 cup of cubed cheddar
Mix canned cream of celery soup according to directions and mix into the ham and potatoes and cheese. Or, make your own cream of celery soup.

Homemade Cream of Celery Soup
1 stalk of celery, chopped
1 small-medium onion, chopped
2 tblsp butter
2 tblsp flour
1 ½ cup milk

Melt butter in a pan, add onion and celery and sauté for about four minutes. Add flour, mix and cook for a couple of minutes until the flour is completely incorporated into the butter. Then add milk slowly, stirring until it becomes slightly thickened and bubbly. Pour this over the casserole. Bake at 350F until bubbly and beginning to brown on top, about 45 minutes.

Once you're down to the hambone with a few bits of meat still clinging, you can make stock as above. Split pea soup made with this broth is fabulous. Or you can throw in a can of beans or some lentils, a few chopped or diced vegetables, and a couple of herbs, and inside 25 minutes, you've got a meal.

Ham Bone Split Pea Soup

6 cups ham stock
1 medium onion, diced
1- 15 oz. bag split peas
1 large carrot, chopped
two cloves of garlic, mashed or minced
freshly ground pepper

You probably won't need salt. Simmer for 35-45 minutes until peas are melted and smooth. Stir periodically; you may need to add a little water if it gets too thick. Delicious and satisfying on a rainy evening with garlic toast.

Quesadillas:

There's a whole world of stuff you can stuff between two tortillas (or in the middle of a big one folded in half like an omelet). Slightly sautéed broccoli, onion and carrot with cheddar. Leftover roasted, grilled or barbequed chicken, sautéed poblanos, onions and seasoning with salsa on the side. Black beans, peppers, corn and Monterey Jack cheese. Sautéed greens (kale, mustard, whatever) with garlic, onions and plenty of cracked pepper with gruyere. Mushrooms sautéed with shallots and fresh thyme and brie. Shredded bits of leftover beef with roasted peppers and cheddar. Bits of leftover fish with a bit of salsa, white wine, cilantro and feta. Leftover turkey with Swiss cheese and cranberry chutney. Mango, pork , mozzarella and squash flowers. Pineapple, leftover grilled chicken breast and leftover grilled veggies with mozzarella. Crab, scallion, a tiny bit of chipotle or Old Bay seasoning and thin-sliced daikon or jicama with a little cream cheese mixed with cheddar, which can stretch a pound of crabmeat deliciously to four people. I once used a quesadilla to turn a half-cup of leftover paella and some grated cheddar into a decent-sized meal for two along with a salad. One of our favorites is shrimp quesadilla accompanied with a nice white wine.

Shrimp Quesadillas

½ pound of shrimp, steamed with Old Bay seasoning, peeled and rough-chopped
4 medium or 2 large white corn or wheat tortillas
½ cup fresh cilantro, chopped
1 ½ cups grated mild cheddar
1 small poblano, chopped
1 sweet red or green pepper, chopped
5 scallions or 1 medium onion chopped
scant bit of dried tomato or salsa, or leftover stewed tomatoes (not runny)
2 tblsp diced celery
splash of white wine
chili flakes or some diced hot pepper
dash of hot sauce
1 tsp chili powder
¼ - ½ tsp cumin
dash of Old Bay
pepper (the salsa and Old Bay probably have enough salt in them)

In olive oil sauté poblano, sweet pepper, scallions or onions, celery and seasonings until nearly soft. Add tomato/salsa or even a squeeze of tomato paste, the wine and shrimp. Stir until just blended. Turn off heat and prepare the pan in which you'll fry the quesadillas.

In a clean, large non-stick pan on medium-high heat, pour in a little olive oil and heat until it shimmers. Take two medium-sized tortillas or one large. Lay one in the pan (if you use the large tortilla, it helps to sort of hang one half up along the pan's side which makes it cook less and is easier to fold over.). The tortilla should immediately sizzle some. Working fairly quickly, sprinkle 1/3 cup of the cheese over the surface of the tortilla (or sprinkle 1/3 cup over half of the large tortilla). The cheese acts as glue (and tastes good). Spread some of the filling over the cheese, then add some more cheese and either flop the second tortilla on it and press down, or fold the second half of the large one over and press down. Fry until the outside is golden and crispy and cheese is melted. (This will take only a minute or two). Then turn over the quesadilla carefully to brown on the other side. (I've 'flipped' more than one and ended up with a mess of filling all over the stove. Slow learner.). Cut into wedges and serve. Salsa verde or sliced avocado drizzled with lime or guacamole can be nice accompaniments.

http://allrecipes.com/Recipe/Asparagus-and-Goat-Cheese-Quesadillas/Detail.aspx
http://allrecipes.com/Recipe/Santa-Fe-Veggie-Quesadillas/Detail.aspx
http://allrecipes.com/Recipe/Quesadillas-I/Detail.aspx
http://allrecipes.com/Recipe/Andouille-and-Poblano-Quesadillas/Detail.aspx
http://www.cooks.com/rec/doc/0,2357,154176-238204,00.html

MAIN MEAL SALADS

Main-meal salads like French lentil and spiced roasted butternut squash with goat cheese or red-and-green cabbage salad with heat-crusted pecans are terrific in either warm or cold weather.

http://www.bonappetit.com/recipe/quinoa-tabbouleh
www.epicurious.com
http://allrecipes.com/recipes/everyday-cooking/Vegetarian/Top.aspx
http://www.vegetariantimes.com/recipes/

TO OUR READERS:

We hope your individual journey is as good as it can possibly be. If this book was helpful to you, we'd appreciate your giving it a review online at Amazon:

on the OK Now What website:

www.oknowwhat.net

on the Head to Wind Publishing website:

www.headtowindpublishing.com

If on the other hand, you were hoping to learn other things that we failed to cover here, we'd appreciate your letting us know via the OK Now What? website

www.oknowwhat.net

where you'll find stories, articles, resources, and downloads of the checklists as well as an interactive blog that will let us help to either answer questions, or at least guide you to where you might find answers. There you can also share your own stories for the encouragement or instruction of others. We're all in this together.

OK, Why the Red Bike?

Because a bicycle represents a lot of things simultaneously: movement, switching gears (though ours doesn't have any, just in case anyone's looking and is a stickler for that particular detail), pausing on the road to take stock of where you are and where you are going from here. It represents the immediacy of a short journey as well as the journey of a lifetime. It signifies a pause to look back at where you have been with your dying loved one as well as a look forward to where you could be going once they have gone. It can represent moving into a new relationship with the deceased and into other relationships in your life.

> A bike implies transition and forward motion, but it doesn't move on its own. We need to get on and pedal; it's up to us to use our energies, our intent to keep it (and ourselves) going. The effort builds muscles, both physical and emotional, and takes us out into the world.

Why red? Because it's bright and therefore stands out as our individual lives stand out for each of us. Because that vibrant red evokes a range of strong emotions including love, passion, sensitivity, as well as rage, anger, courage, strength, and determination. It therefore encompasses the gamut of emotions a caregiver experiences. Also, we chose a red bicycle because we emphatically did not want to evoke the kind of blue-sky-and-dove coupled with choirs-of-angels look that is often associated with this subject. Also, as a practical matter, red stands out on a bookshelf and we wanted the book to stand out visually.

The red bike on the cover represents a vivid passage in life, not always smooth, often fraught with effort, but inevitable and with its own rewards.

Why We Wrote The Book

Sue Collins:

The motivation for writing this book is partly out of my amazement of the expectations of the caregivers I've met, and partly out of the frustration of the caregiver's lack of knowledge of what their loved one is going through, especially emotionally and spiritually. To quote my friend, Carole Connolly, "What greater significance can you put into someone's life than to be a part of their last experience on earth"? We (hospice staff) do our best to make this as good and special as it can be by helping with the difficulties, the decisions and validating their choices. It is very gratifying to watch people grow and transform and have a better understanding of life and death and of themselves.

What matters most? I know I have made a difference in many lives, but I also know that I have been part of something much bigger than myself, and I respect that. I remember conversations more clearly in this work than any other part of life. It is all very intimate and personal, and it makes me feel good about what I am doing.

Nancy Taylor Robson:

I wrote this with Sue because it felt right. It's actually probably as simple, and perhaps as complex as that. I've lived the difference that sitting at the bedside of a loved one, whether it's a family member or friend, can make to them, to the primary caregiver and to myself. I've learned to be calm in the face of the inevitable, and believe that however much we rage against the dying of the light (as I believe we should), it will come for each of us. Being a quiet presence, and effectively helping in whatever way is needed both by the dying and by their caregiver benefits them and me. It makes me a better, kinder person, and more keenly aware that life here is precious.

Acknowledgements

Sue: I am grateful for my hospice team, who taught me the ground work and allowed me at times to fumble and learn, just as you the reader will no doubt experience very valuable learning. I want to thank Mary Williams for sharing the honesty her children taught her and for teaching us the value of a smile. To Linda Oberlin, who travels through life with dignity and poise despite the bumpy times. Everybody needs a friend like Cheryl Hodgson. I am thankful to Allen Polansky, who took a risk and was forever changed. To Tina Maggio for allowing us to use the profound poem her daughter Rachel Gillotti wrote after her father died, a testimony to Tina's parenting.

I want to thank Kelly for introducing me to Nancy Robson. The birth of this book took place during our first meeting over lunch. We were both present in the moment, immediately clicked, and both walked away with potential chapter titles and a new friendship. I am grateful to Nancy for introducing me to Lotte Bowie, who listened to our ideas for a book cover then gave it life. Her web design is perfect for this book; another friendship is born. And I want to thank my husband, Ken Collins, for reading the manuscript, for being supportive and for patiently listening to 30 years of 'my hospice stories.'

Nancy and Sue: Thanks also to Helen Noble, Ben Brack, Mary Ann Bowers, and Alan Polansky as well as all those, who chose to remain anonymous, for sharing your experiences for this book. You've opened your homes and hearts to us and we will always be grateful. Thanks to Helen Noble for taking time from a demanding medical practice to do interviews with Nancy, then to read the manuscript and offer suggestions and insights. Thanks to Gary Robson, whose line-by-line proofreading is often vital, always helpful and usually thought provoking, and to journalist and writer, Melissa MacIntire, for valuable suggestions in addition to careful proofreading. And many thanks to Lotte Bowie of Loblolly Productions for inspired book cover design, website design and friendship and for her graceful perseverance through a terrifying accident that could have taken her life. Thanks also to her husband and collaborative partner, Walter Bowie for making our photo sessions fun. And thanks to Margie Elsberg of Elsberg Associates, whose expertise, given with generosity and humor, urges us on. Thanks for being part of the team.

Nancy Taylor Robson is the author of three other books: **Woman in the Wheelhouse** (Tidewater Publishing 1985, reissued in paperback by Head to Wind Publishing 2013), **Course of the Waterman** (River City Publishing 2004), and **A Love Like No Other: Abigail and John Adams, A Modern Love Story** (Head to Wind Publishing, 2012). All are available on Amazon.

http://www.amazon.com/s/ref=nb_sb_noss_1?url=search-alias%3Daps&field-keywords=nancy+taylor+robson